I0569461

The Edge
of
Enough

Where Wanting More Meets the Courage
to Love Yourself Like It Matters (It Does)

Anne Webb, MA, LCMHC

The Edge of Enough: Where Wanting More Meets the Courage to Love Yourself Like It Matters *(It Does)*

© Copyright <<2025>> Anne Webb, MA, LCMHC

All rights reserved. No part of this publication may be reproduced, distributed or transmitted in any form or by any means, including photocopying, recording, or other electronic or mechanical methods, without the prior written permission of the publisher, except in the case of brief quotations embodied in critical reviews and certain other noncommercial uses permitted by copyright law.

Although the author and publisher have made every effort to ensure that the information in this book was correct at press time, the author and publisher do not assume and hereby disclaim any liability to any party for any loss, damage, or disruption caused by errors or omissions, whether such errors or omissions result from negligence, accident, or any other cause.

Adherence to all applicable laws and regulations, including international, federal, state and local governing professional licensing, business practices, advertising, and all other aspects of doing business in the US, Canada or any other jurisdiction is the sole responsibility of the reader and consumer.

Neither the author nor the publisher assumes any responsibility or liability whatsoever on behalf of the consumer or reader of this material. Any perceived slight of any individual or organization is purely unintentional.

The resources in this book are provided for informational purposes only and should not be used to replace the specialized training and professional judgment of a health care or mental health care professional.

Neither the author nor the publisher can be held responsible for the use of the information provided within this book. Please always consult a trained professional before making any decision regarding treatment of yourself or others.

For more information see website: www.energizewithanne.com
ISBN: 979-8-89694-671-7 - Ebook
ISBN: 979-8-89694-672-4 - Paperback
ISBN: 979-8-89694-673-1 - Hardcover

YOUR COMPANION JOURNAL

Want a place to explore the questions at the end of each chapter a little more deeply? I've created something just for you.

My Reflections from the Edge is a printable companion journal that gathers all of the reflection prompts in one place. It's a space to slow down, listen inward, and connect with the truths rising through *The Edge of Enough*.

You can print it or use it digitally. There is no right pace, no perfect way. Just your presence, your honesty, and your willingness to return to yourself.

This offering is free and available only to readers of this book.

To download the journal, visit:
www.energizewithanne.com/theedgeofenoughjournal

With love,
Anne

DEDICATION

To Mia and Zoe:
my greatest teachers,
fiercest inspirations and most extraordinary gifts
from God

AUTHOR'S NOTE

This book contains references to emotional, physical, sexual, and spiritual abuse, including mentions of rape and trauma. These experiences are shared with care, vulnerability, and the intention to support healing. However, some content may be activating or inappropriate for certain readers depending on age, maturity, or personal experience. Please use discretion.

CONTENTS

PREFACE

(Please read this; it's actually part of the book!)

I first felt the pull to write this book between 1993 and 1995
while pursuing my Master's degree in Counseling.

It was then I began to witness my own story more clearly:
the experiences that had shaped me,
the struggles I had survived,
the resilience that carried me forward.

I use *God* or *the Divine* throughout this book
because those are most meaningful to me.
But please know, you are welcome to translate them
into whatever language speaks to your heart:
Spirit, Universe, Love, the wisdom within.
Whatever name you give to the sacred,
you belong here.

At the time, I thought I understood my journey.
I believed I had arrived at a place where I could translate my pain
into something meaningful for others.

But life had more to teach me.
It would continue to unfold, unravel, and reshape me
in ways I couldn't yet imagine.

The years that followed brought more healing.
More loss.
More transformation.
Each one deepened my understanding of what it truly means to heal.

Healing, I've since learned, is more than mending old wounds.
It's *returning*.
Returning to the self that existed before the noise,
before survival became a default setting,
before I learned to shrink, to please, to prove.

It means learning to love yourself again, or maybe for the first time,
with more than words:
with action.
In the quiet moments.
In the choices no one sees.
In the way you speak to your own heart.

This journey isn't just for the present-day self;
it's for every version of who we've been:
the inner child, the inner teenager, the younger adult,
and the future self still becoming.
Each one carries both wounds and wisdom,
waiting to be acknowledged, loved, and integrated.

True transformation happens when we embrace all of our selves,
offering the care we once needed,
the tenderness we were taught to withhold,
and the radical self-love we are finally learning to extend.

Our inner world is layered and vast.
Within it live the ego and the shadow.

The ego, trying to keep us safe, often clings to control and familiarity.
The shadow holds the parts we've been taught to reject:
shame, fear, need, vulnerability.
Both can hinder us...
or guide us.

They can be enemies.

Or *messengers*.

When we meet them with compassion,
they become allies in our healing,
mirrors showing us where to return
and where to let go.

Throughout my twenty-five-plus years as a mental health therapist,
I have told every client the same thing:
"It is a privilege and an honor to do this work with you."
And I have meant it every time.

Walking alongside others in their healing
has been one of the greatest gifts of my life.

Helping others has also been a way of making sense of my own life—
my own trauma, pain, uncertainty.
It has been my way of transforming something heavy
into wisdom, connection, and purpose.

There was a time I wrote poetry
as a child and as a teenager.
My notebooks were filled with feelings I didn't yet know
how to speak.

But along the way, overcome by shame and silence,
I tore every page and threw it away
so no one would ever see the softness in me.
Not the longing. Not the ache. Not the truth.

With those poems, I lost more than words.
I lost vision.
I lost hope.
I lost any sense of safety I thought I had.

For years, I believed that part of me was gone.
And in many ways, it was.

My voice quieted.
My creativity became a tool for survival:
masking, managing, performing.
It would be decades before I learned to create from wholeness.

But healing has a way of calling us back
to what was buried but not broken.

And in recent years, the words returned.
So did my voice.
So did my ability to create—
not to be seen or saved,
but to be free.

Now, all the parts of me—
the girl who wept in secret,
the teenager who learned to disappear,
the woman who chose to rise—

create together.
And for that, I am eternally grateful.

This book is an extension of my personal, internal alchemy.

It will teach you about breaking generational cycles.
Reclaiming power.
Learning to love yourself
with grace, with truth, and without apology.

You can choose to see what's possible beyond the wound.

You can remember,
unlearn,
let go of what no longer serves you,
and step into the life you were always meant to live.

This is not just my story.
It's an invitation.

As you turn these pages, I invite you to do more than just read.
I invite you to engage
and to allow these words to stir something within you.
I invite you to reflect.
To soften.
To grieve.
To heal.
To remember how deeply worthy of love you've always been.

I invite you to read with compassion,
both for me
and for yourself.

You are not alone in your longing for something more.
You are not alone in your desire to live with freedom, depth, and joy.
And you are not alone in your healing.

Let this book be a guide.
A companion.
A mirror.

Some parts of my story may resonate deeply with you,
affirming something you've always known but never fully articulated.
Other parts may challenge you,
bringing emotion or questions to the surface.

I encourage you to notice what arises.
If a particular passage stirs discomfort, be curious.
If something speaks to you, linger with it.

Move at your own pace.
Pause when you need to.
Read this book once, or return to certain chapters again and again.
Let the words meet you where you are.

There is no rush.
This book carries decades of processing.
You are right on time.

There are layers to all of this:
dots to connect, memories to touch, truths to reclaim.
And it takes patience.
You must meet yourself without pressure or expectation.

Approach it not with "I have to do better,"
but with "I get to love myself."

Reflect on what stirs.
Write. Think. Feel.
Be present in your experience.

Any emotions, resistance, or revelations that surface
are invitations,
opportunities to explore what is asking for your attention.

Take what resonates.
Sit with what stirs you.

And stay open to the possibility
that your greatest struggles
might one day become your greatest source of strength.

Stay open to the possibility
that your pain holds wisdom,
your triggers hold information,
and your struggles have meaning.

Within every challenge lies the potential for transformation,
so approach them all with compassion for every part of yourself.

Healing is about stepping into your highest, most authentic self.
And it's a journey of returning home to the younger selves who still
live within:
the child who felt small,
the teen who longed to be seen,

the young adult searching for meaning,
the future self waiting for you to arrive.

And one more thing I want to acknowledge:
We are always evolving.

By the time this book reaches your hands,
I will likely have lived through more change,
held more insight,
learned more about myself and the world.

That's the nature of life.
Healing is never final;
it is always unfolding.

This is your journey now.
And every step you take, no matter how small,
is leading you closer to the life you are meant to live.

This journey will ask for honesty and courage, yes.
But you don't have to walk it alone.

You are safe.
You are supported.
You are already enough.

This is your path now.
This is your journey home to yourself.

CHAPTER 1

When You Know There's More

*"And the day came when the risk to remain tight in a bud
was more painful than the risk it took to blossom."*
—Anaïs Nin

You wake up exhausted and frustrated. Again.

The weight
of your responsibilities, your expectations,
and the constant giving
is pressing down on you before your feet even touch the floor.

You move through the day on autopilot,
checking the boxes,
meeting others' needs,
pushing through.

And beneath it all, a question quietly echoes:
Is this all there is?

You've worked hard.
Done everything you were "supposed" to do.
And yet, something still feels off.

A quiet ache lingers just beneath the surface:
a longing for something more.

More meaning.
More connection.
More you.

I know this ache.
I know this story.

I lived it for years.
I, too, was stuck in crushing cycles
of exhaustion, self-doubt, and survival.

I, too, was convinced that if I just tried harder, gave more,
or held everything together a little bit longer,
I would finally feel free.

But instead,
I felt more and more disconnected
from myself,
from joy,
from the life I knew I was meant to be living.

And yet, even in my most depleted moments,
there was a part of me that held on to hope like a lifeline.
I whispered prayers.

I dreamed, quietly, of a life that felt more honest, more beautiful, more aligned.

I remember being young
and shrinking as much as I could
so I wouldn't be noticed.

I feared rejection.
And for so long—through childhood and into early adulthood—
I was almost mute where it mattered.
There was no space for me to process out loud,
and I didn't yet have the skills or experience
to name what I was feeling.
I was delayed—
not in depth,
but in voice.

Still, I hesitated,
but I tried
with all I had,
with all I knew.

And decades later,
I found myself hesitating to speak my truth for the exact same reason.
That part of me was still there: quiet, protective,
afraid to let me be seen.

Some aspects of yourself may also question whether you are worthy
of this journey.

This resistance is natural.
Many of us have internalized beliefs that keep us stuck in old ways of being.

Some of us feel an unconscious pull to repeat familiar patterns,
even when they no longer serve us.

But if you still hear the quiet whispers
of other parts—perhaps of your soul—
urging you to break free...
no matter how quiet they are, how inconsistent,
if they are there,
then you have hope,
because you can learn to listen
and, with them, create a change.

Looking Back to Move Forward

I had done everything I knew to do.
I pursued education,
built a career,
and raised my daughters,
all of which brought me joy and satisfaction.

Yet the restlessness and longing for more remained.

Life after divorce,
much like the rest of life,
offered no clear path forward.

One daughter just three years old,
the other only five months,
and no guarantees that doing the "right" things would lead to
fulfillment.

I was always in motion,
always pushing through,
but never fully arriving.

And this wasn't just my struggle.
It was a pattern woven through generations.

A legacy of pain, survival instincts, and inherited beliefs about love,
worth, and sacrifice.

I had absorbed those unspoken wounds deeply,
carrying what had gone unresolved before me.

And once I saw that pattern, I felt a profound responsibility
and a passion
to break free of it,
not just for myself,
but for my daughters
and for the generations to come.

I longed to live from a place of freedom and ease.
There is no life without challenge,
but I could still find a way to breathe without bracing,
to love without proving,
to rest without guilt.

But the path forward felt obscured,
like I was drifting through a vast ocean,
constantly moving,
never truly arriving.

Healing wasn't linear.
It was long, layered, and unpredictable.

I had spent years carrying the weight of childhood wounds,
perfectionism, and self-abandonment,
always searching for approval,
always trying to be enough.

I had absorbed the silence of those who turned away,
the expectations of a faith that taught me I had to earn love,
and the unspoken grief passed down through generations.

But something in me kept seeking.

And one night,
staring at the ceiling in the quiet dark,
I heard it again,
a familiar whisper:

What if life could be different?

I'd heard it before,
but this time, it was stronger.
Was it only a question...
or was it a knowing?

It wasn't that I had avoided change.
I had always been searching, learning, and growing,
always reaching for more.

But we can only see a small fraction of reality
until something shifts.

And that night, something did.

I now knew I was breaking free for more than myself.
I was breaking free for every version of me that had carried us this far
and for everyone who had been taught that survival was the only
option.

Lying in the dark,
I thought of them:
the little girl who scanned the room before speaking,
the teenager who tried so hard to be enough,
the young woman who carried more than she ever should have.

I saw them clearly.
I felt their presence.
And I realized something...

They weren't just memories.
They were *me*.

And they were still waiting
to be seen,
to be heard,
to be loved.

So I began writing to them,
telling them what they always needed to hear.

I couldn't fix the past,
but I could honor the ones who'd helped me get to where I am now:
the ones who'd endured,
the ones who'd dreamed,
the ones who'd held on,
the ones who'd made undoing—regenerating—possible.

That night, I began to rewrite our story.

To My Child Self

Sweet girl, I see you.

I see the way your wide, curious eyes search the world
for love,
for safety,
for a place where you can simply be.

I see how hard you try
to be small,
to be good,
to be quiet,
believing that if you're just enough in all the right ways,
the storm will settle.

I see how you scan the room,
reading the energy before speaking,
always preparing for what might come next.

Will there be yelling?
A slammed door?
The sound of something breaking:
a dish, a promise, a bone?

Will he drive too fast again,
rage rising like a wave you can't stop?

You never know who might be hurt
in any number of ways:
physically,

emotionally,
silently.

So you've learned to stay ready.
To freeze.
To disappear.

Thank you for doing the best you can to stay safe
in all the ways you know how.

You are so smart.
So sensitive.
So deeply attuned to everything around you.

I see you, too:
standing on your head,
hanging upside down,
twisting yourself into shapes
just to feel something different,
to find some kind of calm.

You don't know it yet,
but you are listening to your body.
You are trying to regulate what feels overwhelming.
Your body knows,
even when your mind doesn't.

I know how much you hate the haircuts,
the boy clothes that never feel like you.

You want to be a girl,
to be seen as a girl,
but it's humiliating when people mistake you for a boy.

And deep down,
you also know that being a girl isn't safe in your home.
It isn't safe to be anything in your home.

You feel the shame before you even have words for it,
rushing to get dressed before your dad comes home,
avoiding his presence like it might swallow you whole.

And then comes her voice—your mother's voice:
"If you don't fix your relationship with your father,
you'll never be able to love a man."

You are only eight.
But you're already carrying the weight of everyone else's story.

And at night,
when he tears the buttons from his pajamas while praying—
calling it holy,
calling it spiritual—
you sit with the confusion,
the fear,
the ache of it all.

And in the morning,
you and your sister quietly sew them back on,
as if this is normal,
as if this burden is yours to carry.

I'm so sorry, sweet one.
That is not okay.
You don't deserve any of it.

But, my love,
you are already worthy.
And you were never meant to carry so much.

You were never meant to earn love
by being pleasing,
perfect,
or the fixer.

You were never meant to be the one keeping everyone safe.
That was never your job.

You are a bright light,
a force of nature,
a beautiful soul who was born to be free,
to run wild,
to be held—
not to hold the burdens of others.

I know the pain feels big right now.
But the world is so much bigger
than the hurt that surrounds you.

There will be moments of softness,
glimpses of wonder,
places where your spirit will feel safe enough to exhale.

Hold on to those moments, sweet one.
Because one day,
you will create a life filled with them.

One day,
you will know what it means to be free.

Until then,
keep dancing in the wind.
Keep talking to the trees
and feeling God in the quiet places.
Keep dreaming of what could be,
because you are not wrong for wanting more.

To My Teenage Self

Oh, my brave, strong girl.
You have carried more
than most will ever know.
You've learned how to mask the pain,
to push through,
to keep smiling
even when you feel like screaming inside.

You tell yourself that if you can just be better,
smarter,
more accommodating,
maybe then,
maybe finally,
you'll belong.
Maybe then,
someone will see you,
choose you,
stay with you.

I know how much you want to feel like yourself,
to express who you are,
but even your appearance isn't fully your own:
the perms you don't want,
the constant pressure to fall in line,
to obey without resistance.

Not being compliant means worse than disapproval;
it means punishment.
It means violence
and fear.
So you submit.
And in doing so,
you lose yourself a little more.

But I want to cheer you on for everything you do:
for working hard to buy your own clothes,
for piecing together outfits that feel like you,
for recognizing what you need
and making it happen
in the smallest, most powerful ways.
That is you beginning to take up space,
even when the world tells you to stay small.

You feel unsafe in your own skin,
self-conscious even in the shower,
where the bathroom window remains uncovered,
exposing you,
leaving you unprotected.
Still, you take so many showers,
hoping to wash it all down the drain.
Hoping to ground yourself,
free yourself,
come back home to a body you've been taught not to trust.

There's been no television,
not since you were two.
No music permitted, except the kind deemed "holy."
No language for your confusion.
No foundation of love or communication
to make any of it make sense.
Only control,
silence,
and so much shame.

You're growing up inside purity culture,
where pleasure is sinful
and anything that brings joy is suspect.
Where everything is motivated by fear—
especially fear of your own body,
your desires,
your voice.

You've been taught to suppress instead of feel,
to obey instead of explore.
You feel suffocated,
strange,
cut off.

But I need you to hear me now:
You are not too much.
You are enough.
You always have been.
You don't have to work so hard
to earn your place in the world.
You are already worthy of the kind of love
that doesn't require you to shrink.

I know how much it hurts
when you feel invisible.
But their inability to love you
the way you deserve
is not proof that you are unlovable.
It's proof
of their limitations,
not your worth.

They love from their wounds,
not from wholeness.

You are worthy of friendships that don't drain you,
relationships that don't ask you to prove your value,
spaces where you don't have to apologize for existing.

Please stop being so hard on yourself.
You are not failing
just because you don't have all the answers.
You are learning.
You are growing.
You are becoming.
And all of that takes time.

You've never fit neatly into any box,
and that's not a flaw.
It's a gift.
Your sensitivity,
your depth,
your wild heart—
they were never meant to be contained.

Please don't trade your truth
for belonging with people who ask you to become someone
you're not.

Keep dreaming wild dreams.
Keep listening to the voice inside you,
even when it trembles.
Keep choosing yourself
in small, brave ways.
That's how the light gets in.
That's how you find your way home.

Thank you
for trying so hard,
even when you hate yourself,
even when you feel like a failure.
You are never failing.
You are surviving.

I promise you,
one day,
you will look back at this version of yourself
and feel so proud of her.
You'll thank her for holding on through it all,
for keeping the spark alive,
for continuing to believe.

And one day,
you won't just be getting through the days anymore.
You'll be thriving.
And it will be so, so good.

To My Young Adult Self

You kind, compassionate, determined, hopeful woman!

I want to begin by saying this:
You aren't failing.
You are doing your best with what you have.
And I hold you now with nothing but love.

I honor you for all the ways you think you have to prove yourself:
for loving people who can't love you back,
for staying in places that dim your light,
for saying yes when your soul whispers no.

I know why you try so hard to be who everyone else needs you to be:
because you think that's what love requires,
because you're afraid of being left,
because you don't yet know you are already enough.

And I extend so much grace and compassion to you.

But I also want to thank you.
Thank you for your courage.
Thank you for waking up every morning
and choosing to stand up for yourself,
both in big ways
and in small moments.
Thank you for choosing healing,
even when it feels like walking into the unknown
with no map and no guarantee.

I see the emotional anorexia you're surviving,
the deep lack of nourishment of every kind.
I see the confusion around your body,
the shame that was never yours to carry,
the fat-burning pills your mother gave you
when you weighed barely over a hundred pounds.

I see the harshness you've turned inward,
the way you punish your body with expectations
and slowly—so slowly—
are learning to listen instead.
You've started softening.
You've begun feeding yourself love
in small, quiet ways.

You've married before really getting to know yourself,
and you've tripped right into old patterns:
patterns of loyalty, of sacrifice,
of losing yourself to survive.

And still,
you want more.
You want healing.
You want truth.

You're going to grad school to build a career,
but also to grow,
to evolve,
to help others heal in the ways you're still learning to heal yourself.

You're living with endometriosis,
wondering if you'll ever become a mother.
You wait.
You endure.

And eventually,
you're raising two amazing daughters on your own
and giving them the gift of presence.
You're a mom who never stops learning,
who keeps believing in more,
for herself and for them.

You've begun breaking the cycle.
You've begun rewriting the story.
You were the first to say, "This ends with me."

Even when you are depleted,
even when you are running on fumes,
you keep going.
You keep rescuing your parents in moments of crisis,
terrified that if you don't,
someone might not survive.

It's never enough.
And that's when you'll start questioning the belief
that you are not enough.
That belief will begin to crack.
And something new will begin to grow in its place.

You show up with remnants of self-loathing
and a rising determination to uncover your worth.
You don't always know how,
but you try.
You keep taking steps forward,
falling down,
getting back up.
You are relentless.

There are nights the darkness nearly swallows you,
moments when the thoughts turn sharp,
when escape whispers louder than hope.
You've even toyed with the idea—once, maybe twice—
but something in you always pulls you back.
You feel the feelings.
You wrestle the demons.
And you win every single time.
Because you were meant for more.

You are fiercely independent,
capable,
creative.
There is nothing you can't do.

You want love—real love—
but you aren't going to settle.
You'll begin setting boundaries.
You'll begin using your voice.

Yes, you are still naive sometimes,
still tender,
still operating from old stories.

But even the missteps are sacred.
Even the endings are beginnings.

I know how exhausted you've been,
how heavy it feels to carry the expectations,
the roles,
the unspoken agreements
that were never yours to hold.

I know how deeply you long for freedom,
for a life that feels like yours.

And here's the truth, love:
That life is coming.
It's already on its way.

One day,
you will stop settling.
You will no longer abandon yourself
in exchange for love,
acceptance,
or approval.

You will trust yourself enough to let go of it all:
undeserving people,
old identities, limiting beliefs,
and the story that says your worth
is tied to what you do rather than who you are.

You will look in the mirror
and recognize yourself:
no longer who you think you should be,
but the woman you always have been.

So keep finding wonder in the stars
and all of nature.
Keep journaling and learning.
Keep setting boundaries,
both for yourself
and for others.

Keep hiking.
Keep moving your body with care.
Keep feeding yourself well—
good food, yes,
but also gentleness.
Keep reading books that open your heart
and speaking words that reveal the truth.

And please
extend grace and compassion to yourself.

You deserve softness.
You deserve ease.
You deserve to be loved without condition.

I love you.
I believe in you.
And I promise
this story ends in joy.

Turning Point

I see them now:
the little girl,
the teenager,
the young woman.

More than memories,
they are me.

And as I step forward,
I do not leave them behind.
I carry them with me:
whole, honored, and free.

No longer proving,
no longer running.
Just becoming.

I interrupted the old pattern of self-abandonment
and began to trust—
for the first time—
that I was already enough,
that I was whole,
that I was worthy of love and healing.
That belief shifted my inner world
and changed the course of my life.

I became a therapist not because I had it all figured out by then,
but because I still had questions.
I was searching.

And I wanted to help others,
even as I was still learning how to help myself.

That was one step,
an important one.
But the deeper work would come later.

Through journaling, through reflection,
through years of survival and slow reckoning,
the truth began to rise—
and eventually, the letters came.
The words I had never spoken
began to shape the healing I had longed for.

Those letters did not arrive at the beginning;
they were born from everything I had lived.
They gave me insight,
but more than that,
they gave me a return.

But that wasn't the end of the journey.

I felt a call to move beyond the therapy room
and into more expansive ways of guiding transformation.
That call led me to coaching,
energy healing,
mentorship,
and writing.

As my work began to deepen,
I began to understand that
the emotional, physical, and energetic wounds I carried

weren't really obstacles.
They were gateways.

Each one held wisdom.
Each one taught me compassion.
Each one gave me tools I could pass on to others.

My ongoing healing journey became the foundation
for how I now help others navigate their own.

I began turning inward more intentionally,
releasing old patterns,
reclaiming my power,
and aligning my choices with my deepest truth.

I had gone from surviving
and performing
to beginning to live with intention.

And I realized something powerful:

The real barrier wasn't the world outside of me.
It was the old stories I had been told
and that I was still telling myself.

Stories that said my worth was tied to what I did.
That if I stopped striving, I would disappear.
That safety meant silence.
That being seen was dangerous.
That love was conditional.
That freedom was selfish.

Those stories shaped my decisions,
my relationships,
and my capacity to trust.

And if I wanted something different,
I had to rewrite the script.

So I did.

By renewing my mind,
by challenging every thought rooted in scarcity, fear, and self-doubt,
I began to reprogram the way I saw myself,
others,
and the world around me.

And this journey,
this transformation,
is for more
than just me.

It's for my daughters,
who deserve to see their mother live fully and freely.

It's for every client,
student,
and soul I get to walk alongside.

It's for the ones who are ready to break old cycles
and create something radically new.

Breaking generational patterns isn't easy.
On the one hand,
it requires grace, grit, and resilience.

On the other,
it demands surrender,
trust,
and flow.

It requires relinquishment of the illusion of control
and the deep, embodied knowing
that we are divinely guided and protected.

We must soften where we've armored up.
We must root into something deeper than certainty: faith.
We must let healing unfold in divine timing,
even when we can't yet see the outcome.

That said,
I have faced consequences.

Things I missed.
Years I spent in struggle.
Seasons that felt lost
to burnout,
to overgiving,
to relationships that blurred my voice,
to longing that had nowhere safe to land.

And still,
I choose to believe I am on time.

Nothing has been wasted.
Everything is working out for me
in ways I can't yet fully see.

Because when we choose healing—
both to break generational patterns
and to discover and love our authentic selves—
we transform more than our own lives;
we create a ripple that touches generations.

I wrote these words in a moment of stillness,
and they've become a personal truth I return to again and again:

This is how we heal the world:
by embodying love from the inside out.

These words have become my compass.

I believe that as we learn to love ourselves—
truly, fiercely, tenderly—
we change everything.

One person's healing becomes a mirror,
a light,
a spark.

And when one of us changes,
the world changes.

The life we ache for isn't somewhere out there.
It already lives within us,
waiting to be remembered and reclaimed.

And that journey
is worth every single step.

Why We Disconnect from Ourselves

Before we can remember who we are,
we have to understand why we forgot.

From the time we're born,
we begin learning about the world
and about ourselves
from the people and environments around us.

The way love is given (or withheld),
the way safety is modeled (or not),
and the way we're responded to when we express emotion
all send messages that shape how we see ourselves.

Most of us weren't taught how to trust ourselves.
Instead,
we learned to become what others needed us to be.

Maybe you were praised when you were quiet,
polite,
or helpful.
Maybe you were corrected when you had needs,
opinions,
or big emotions.

Maybe you learned that it was safer to please others
than to speak up.
Maybe you started performing,
fixing,
or perfecting to keep the peace.

Over time,
many of us disconnect from who we really are.
This doesn't mean we're weak or broken;
we're simply wired to seek connection.

As Dr. Gabor Maté explains,
when authenticity feels like a threat to connection,
we learn to abandon ourselves
to stay close to others.
We trade truth for attachment.
And we call it love.[1]

When being our true selves risks compromising the love or
safety we need,
we learn to sacrifice authenticity to stay connected.

This makes sense, especially when we're children.
Abandoning parts of ourselves often helped us gain something:
protection, attention, belonging, or approval.
Maybe it helped us avoid punishment.
Maybe it made the adults around us feel more comfortable.
Maybe it was the only way we knew how to stay connected.

But the cost adds up.

That disconnection from ourselves often shows up later in life as
burnout,
anxiety,
resentment,

---

1 Gabor Maté, *When the Body Says No: The Cost of Hidden Stress* (Toronto: Vintage
Canada, 2011).

people-pleasing,
overworking,
or just the feeling that something isn't quite right,
even if things look fine on the outside.

Eventually,
many of us reach a point where something no longer fits.
Life may look "fine" on the outside,
but inside, there's a growing ache,
a quiet voice asking,

Who am I underneath all these masks?
Is this the life I want to keep living?

That voice is an invitation,
not to become someone new,
but to return to who we've always been underneath the noise,
the roles,
and the conditioning.

What Creates Change

Change doesn't just happen by accident.

It starts with awareness:
that quiet, sometimes disorienting moment
when the noise fades just enough
for truth to rise.

Awareness is the space between autopilot and choice.
It might show up as discomfort,
an ache you can no longer ignore,
or a moment of stillness that startles you awake.

It might say,
Is this the story I still want to live?
Is it time to write a new one?

But awareness is only the beginning.

In my experience,
transformation tends to begin when three things come together:

1. A Breaking Point
You realize something isn't working.
It might feel like burnout,
a crisis (physical, emotional, mental, or spiritual),
restlessness,
or a quiet but persistent ache.
You only know you can't keep doing things the same way.

2. A Spark of Courage
Even the smallest flicker of hope
can open a new door:
the willingness to try something different,
to rest instead of push,
to speak when silence feels safer,
to believe, even briefly,
that something more is possible.

3. A Commitment to Yourself
You don't need to do everything perfectly.
You just need to return—
to yourself,
to the work,
to the truth—
again and again,
even when it's hard.
Especially when it's hard.

I can't count the number of times I've heard clients
and other people in my life say,
"This is just how I am."

They wear it like a badge of finality,
as if their past, their conditioning,
or their circumstances have carved their identity in stone.

But that belief is a trap.

Yes, we are shaped by our experiences,
but we are not bound by them.

The moment we become aware,
we also become responsible for what we do with that awareness.

That's where the spark comes in.
That's where the commitment begins.

We get to choose—
repeatedly—
who we want to become.

Choosing Your Path

The truth is,
both changing and staying the same are hard.

It's hard to set boundaries,
to disappoint others,
to step into the unknown.

And it's also hard to stay stuck in patterns that drain you,
to keep feeling unfulfilled,
unseen,
disconnected.

Both paths carry weight.
One asks you to stay small.
The other asks you to grow.

Neither is easy,
but only one leads to freedom.

You get to decide which path you're willing to walk.
You get to choose your hard.

You Were Always on Your Way Home

You've made it here, to this edge:
the edge of enough.
This is where survival begins to give way to awareness,
where the ache for more becomes a map.

There's nothing wrong with you for wanting a different life.
That longing isn't a flaw;
it's a compass.

And the more you listen,
the more you'll remember:
You were never lost.
You were always on your way home.

Invitation

Before you begin,
pause.

Notice what your body is asking for.
Do you need a sip of water?
A nourishing snack?
A stretch?
A few deep breaths?

Tend to yourself
with gentleness.

Then find a comfortable place to land,
a space where you can exhale.
This is your time.

No pressure.
No performance.
Just presence.

Reflection Prompts

Let these meet you where you are.
You're not searching for answers;
you're remembering what's true.

1. What dreams or desires have you set aside,
    believing they were too much
    or out of reach?
    Are any of them still quietly calling to you?

2. Where in your life are you simply surviving
    rather than fully living?
    What would thriving look and feel like
    in those spaces?

3. What old beliefs or roles
    have shaped how you show up in the world?
    Which ones are you ready to question...
    or release?

4. When do you feel most disconnected from yourself?
    What helps you come home
    to who you really are?

5. If you stopped performing
    and started trusting your enoughness,
    what might become possible?

Next Steps

This is where insight becomes action:
small, doable ways to begin living what you're learning.

You don't need to do them all.
Choose what resonates
and leave the rest.
Don't think of these as tasks to check off.
They're invitations to apply what you're uncovering,
gently, honestly, at your own pace.

Let your insight become an act of love.
Small steps make big shifts over time.

- Choose one area of your life
  where you've been going through the motions.
  Ask yourself,
  What's one small step
  I can take toward truth or presence here?
- Start a "remembering" journal.
  Capture moments
  when you feel most like yourself,
  unfiltered and without performance.
- Set one micro-boundary this week
  that honors your energy:
  a simple no,
  a pause,
  a request.

- Reconnect with something
  your younger self loved:
  a song, a tree, a practice,
  a part of you that's still waiting.

Integration

You're not behind.
You're becoming.

You don't have to rush.
You don't have to know what's next.
You just have to stay
with yourself.

The spark is already there.
The path will rise to meet you,
one breath,
one truth,
one brave step at a time.

CHAPTER 2

Honoring Who We Had to Be

"You either walk inside your story and own it,
or you stand outside your story and hustle for your worthiness."
—Brené Brown

Where We've Been, Where We're Going

In Chapter 1, we began to notice the ache:
a quiet knowing
that we were made for more
than just getting by.

We started to listen inward,
to soften the old stories,
to remember what got buried
beneath all the roles we played.

But before we return
to who we really are,
we must gently meet
the selves we became to survive.

The Driven Doer.
The Sensitive Soul.
The Heart-Centered Harmonizer.
The Lost Child.
The Quiet Seeker.
The Vivacious Visionary.
The Legacy Transformer.

Or maybe someone else entirely.

These identities aren't labels.
They're starting points,
maps of how we coped,
how we stayed connected,
how we made it through.

Now, we honor them.
And we ask,
What still serves us?
What are we ready to release?

This is where transformation begins:
with awareness,
with compassion,
with choice.

From Survival Mode to Self-Awareness

It starts as a quiet discomfort,
a growing sense that something is missing.

Life begins to feel out of alignment,
disconnected,
or unsustainable.

That inner stirring is an invitation
to pause,
to listen,
and to ask a different question.

Some ignore it. They stay in survival mode for decades.
They numb out,
push harder,
or wait for a breaking point.

The truth is,
we all have the choice to wake up, whenever we like.

We all have the ability
to step into the driver's seat of our own life
and start making intentional decisions
that reflect who we really are.

That's where healing begins.

Recognizing Survival Identities

Once we begin to wake up,
really wake up,
we start to notice the patterns we've been living out for years.

These patterns are often formed early,
shaped by family dynamics,
unspoken rules,
personal experiences,
and the environments we moved through.

In my personal and professional experience,
I've seen several common survival identities show up again and again:

the Driven Doer, the Sensitive Soul, the Heart-Centered
Harmonizer, the Lost Child, the Quiet Seeker, the Vivacious
Visionary, and the Legacy Transformer.

These are all reflections of deeply ingrained strategies,
often invisible,
that once helped us navigate pain or uncertainty.

They helped us cope.
They helped us feel safe, accepted, or in control.

But now,
they may be keeping us stuck in old behaviors that do more harm
than good.

You might see yourself clearly in one.
You might recognize pieces of yourself in several.
Or you may feel like you don't fit into any of them,
and that's okay, too.

The goal isn't to identify with a role.
It's to become aware of how you've adapted
so you can choose what still serves you
and release what you're ready to release.

Ways We Adapt to Stay Safe:
The Survival Identities

The following seven poems describe survival identities I've identified,
patterns many of us develop early in life to stay safe,
to belong,
to avoid conflict,
or to earn love.

These identities are rooted in protection.
They were wise when first adopted,
but over the years,
they can keep us disconnected from our true needs,
our voice,
our wholeness.

The point of this exercise is not to feel shame.
You simply want to see yourself clearly,
with compassion,
with curiosity,
with the possibility of choosing something new.

The Driven Doer

You're the high achiever,
the go-getter,
the one who always finds a way to get things done.

You've likely been praised for your performance,
your discipline,
your results,
your ability to hold it all together
even under pressure.

Somewhere along the way,
accomplishment became safety.
Productivity became identity.
Doing became self-worth.

You've learned to push through exhaustion,
to ignore your limits,
to raise the bar even higher.

There's always more to prove,
more to fix,
more to finish.

But underneath the drive,
there's often anxiety
and fear of slowing down.

A quiet question rises:
Who am I if I'm not achieving?

Eventually,
the pace catches up with you.
You might feel burned out,
disconnected,
or like you're chasing a finish line
that keeps moving out of reach.

You're starting to see
that success doesn't have to come at the cost of peace.
Rest isn't laziness,
and you don't have to earn your worth.

Now,
you're ready to redefine what success means to you,
to create a life where achievement and ease can exist together,
to stop doing just to be valued
and start becoming someone who values themselves.

The Sensitive Soul

You notice the shifts in a room,
the tension under the surface,
the unspoken needs no one names.

You're deeply attuned to the emotions and energy of others.
You feel things intensely,
sometimes before anyone else does.

You've likely been the emotional support for others
for as long as you can remember.
You support.
You give.
You care,
often more than is asked or acknowledged.

And for a while, this worked.
You were praised for being easy, kind, dependable.
People trusted you, leaned on you.
Your sensitivity became your superpower,
a way to stay safe, connected, needed.

But over time,
this constant giving can leave you drained.
You may struggle to ask for what you need.
You may feel responsible for others' feelings
or overwhelmed by the emotional weight you carry.
You don't want to seem selfish,
so you keep showing up for others,
even when you're running on empty.

Sometimes that looks like canceling your plans to support someone else,
or skipping rest or meals to stay available,
or feeling too spent at the end of the day to be present with yourself.
It adds up.

But something inside you is starting to shift.
A whispered question begins to rise:
What if honoring my needs is the most loving thing I can do?

You're beginning to realize that your sensitivity isn't a weakness;
it's a gift.
It's what allows you to sense what others can't,
to hold space, offer empathy, and read between the lines.
And when directed inward,
it becomes a well of intuition, creativity, and deep self-knowing.

It's time to stop abandoning yourself
in the name of caring for others.

Now,
you're ready to reclaim your energy,
set boundaries without guilt,
and reconnect with yourself.
You're learning to lead with compassion—
starting with how you treat yourself.

The Heart-Centered Harmonizer

You're the peacekeeper,
the giver,
the one who smooths things over and makes everyone else feel okay.

You're deeply caring and emotionally attuned,
and you likely learned early on
that keeping the peace meant staying safe.

You prioritize harmony,
often by putting others' comfort above your own.

You say yes when you want to say no.
You shrink your preferences to avoid conflict.
You carry the emotional weight of others quietly and consistently.

Over time,
this can leave you feeling invisible—
resentful, even—
but you worry that speaking up might hurt someone,
that setting boundaries might mean losing connection.

A tender question begins to surface:

What if honoring my truth is the only way to feel truly connected?

You've been trained to put others first—
so much so,
you may not even know what you want anymore.

But you're beginning to realize something:
Peace that comes at the cost of your voice isn't really peace.

Now,
you're ready to honor your own needs, too.

To say what you mean without fear, obligation, or guilt.
To stop abandoning yourself in order to be accepted.
And to learn that true connection includes you.

The Lost Child

You're the quiet one,
the observer,
the one who slipped through the cracks.

You learned to fade into the background,
to be low-maintenance,
self-sufficient,
unseen.

This wasn't because you didn't have needs.
It just felt safer not to reveal them.

You may have grown up in chaos
or around strong personalities.

Maybe attention was unpredictable or unavailable.

So you found comfort in solitude,
books,
music,
nature,
and imagination.

You created your own internal world
where you didn't have to perform, fix, or compete.

But with that invisibility came disconnection.

You got used to not being asked how you felt
or not knowing how to answer when you were.

Even now,
you may hesitate to take up space.

You may downplay your needs
or silence your voice,
unsure if it's safe to be seen.

A gentle question begins to stir:

*What if being seen doesn't threaten my safety but restores my
wholeness?*

Now, part of you is ready to come forward.

To stop fading and start engaging.
To know that your presence matters,
regardless of what you do or don't do
or how easy you are to swallow,
simply for the vibrant and unique person you are.

You're ready to take up space in your own life,
to reconnect with your needs,
your voice,
and your sense of belonging.

The Quiet Seeker

You're thoughtful, intuitive, often introspective.
You may not have been the loudest voice in the room,
but you've always been tuned in, observing, feeling, quietly
questioning.

You've carried a lot inside: emotions you didn't know how to express,
insights that others may not have understood,
longings you weren't sure how to name.

You've always sensed there was something more.
Even if you didn't have the language for it,
you felt it beneath the surface of daily life, behind the noise of
expectations.

You played it safe on the outside,
but inside, you were searching
for meaning, depth, connection.

And yet, for all your seeking, you've held back,
unsure if you're ready,
afraid you won't be received.

A quiet wondering begins to rise:
What if I already hold the answers I've been searching for?

And now, something in you is shifting.

You're ready to stop second-guessing your voice.
You're ready to trust yourself,
to stop just seeking answers
and start living aligned with the wisdom that's always been in you.

The Vivacious Visionary

You're the dreamer,
the creator,
the one with vision and drive.

You've always known there was more available to you,
and you haven't held back.
You've achieved a lot by following that inner pull.

You've built a life that looks successful on the outside.
People admire your energy, your ambition, your ability to make
things happen.

But even with all that momentum, something still feels incomplete.
You've been moving fast, maybe too fast, trying to keep up with your
own potential.

At times, you've chased validation,
looking outward for answers, approval, or direction
while quietly ignoring your inner voice.

A bold question begins to surface:
What if my worth was never tied to what I accomplish?

Now, you're starting to hear it again.

You don't need to prove anything anymore.
You're ready to slow down.
You're not giving up;
you're tuning in.

You're learning to create from alignment instead of pressure.
You're learning to trust your own inner guidance:
your ideas, your body, your energy, your intuition.

You're ready to let your vision be shaped by what feels true,
not just what looks impressive.

Your dreams haven't gone anywhere.
But now, you're creating from wholeness,
from enoughness,
from trust.

The Legacy Transformer

You're the pattern shifter.
You saw what wasn't working and chose to do things differently.

You may have come from a lineage of pain, silence, dysfunction, or unhealed trauma.
You've felt the weight of what was passed down: the beliefs, the behaviors, the emotional inheritance.

Maybe you tried to follow the rules.
Maybe you rebelled.
Either way, you knew one thing deep down: *This cannot continue with me.*

Your life has been shaped by that commitment,
sometimes consciously, sometimes not.

You've carried what others couldn't or wouldn't face.
You've questioned the systems, challenged the narratives, and done the hard work of healing.

It hasn't been easy.
You may feel tired, misunderstood, or alone in your choices.

A sacred question begins to echo:
What if breaking the cycle was always enough—even when no one applauded me for it?

You are not broken; you are brave.

And you are not here just to disrupt.
You are here to rebuild.

Now, you're beginning to integrate,
to choose what to carry forward with intention
and what to lay down for good.

You're creating a new legacy,
as much for those who come after you
as for yourself.

Because you deserve a life that isn't shaped by survival.
You deserve to feel joy, ease, and connection,
and to know that being the one who chose to change was always
enough.

What Unites These Journeys

These survival identities may look different,
but they have a lot in common.

First, there's a deep desire for something more.
Each identity was shaped by a way of coping,
whether that meant overgiving, striving, shutting down, or keeping
the peace.

These strategies helped us feel safe or accepted.
But over time, they can leave us feeling disconnected from who we
really are.

Underneath those patterns,
there's usually a quiet longing:
to feel more alive,
more at ease,
more like ourselves again.

The second thing these identities share is a readiness for change.

Look at the identity or identities that best fit you and ask yourself,

Do these roles still fit?
Do they still serve me?

Even if none of the above patterns feel like a perfect fit, this book still
has something for you.

Whether it's setting boundaries,
healing generational wounds,
slowing down,
or learning to speak up,
there's a shift happening.

People everywhere are starting to see that they don't want to keep
repeating the same patterns.

That's why this book is for anyone who feels tired of living on
autopilot.
It's for anyone who knows, deep down,
that there's more to life than just getting by.

If you've felt stuck in self-doubt,
burned out,
disconnected,
or unsure how to move forward,
you're not alone.

These struggles are real,
but they don't define who you are.

The life you want,
the one that feels aligned and meaningful,
isn't out of reach.

It already lives inside you.
You may have been taught to ignore it,
to push it down,
or to believe it isn't possible.

But it is.

This process takes courage, clarity, and commitment.
But you don't need to do it perfectly.
You don't need to become someone new.

You just need to return to the person you've always been
underneath the noise, the pressure, and the fear.

You won't find a quick fix here,
but you will find a real and lasting shift.

And it starts now.

Acknowledge the Courage It Takes

It takes courage to slow down,
to ask real questions,
and to be honest with yourself.

You're already moving toward change,
even just by showing up here.

This isn't a journey of fixing yourself.
Instead, you are coming home to yourself,
bit by bit,
moment by moment.

You're doing the work.
You're already on your way.

Invitation

Before you begin,
pause.

Notice what your body might need.
A sip of water?
A stretch?
A few slow breaths to settle your energy?

Find a space where you feel supported.
Let this be a soft landing,
not another thing to push through.

Again, you're not here to fix yourself.
You're here to understand yourself more deeply,
with compassion, with honesty, and with choice.

Reflection Prompts

Let these questions guide you inward.
Don't worry about getting it right.
You only need to be honest with yourself and for yourself.

1. Which of the survival identities resonated with you most,
   if any?
   Did one feel especially familiar?
   Or do you see yourself in several?

2. If none of them felt like an exact fit,
   how would you describe the way you adapted to survive?
   What would you name your survival identity?

3. What roles or patterns have helped you feel
   safe, loved, or in control,
   even if they no longer serve you now?

4. Where in your life do you still feel the pull to
   shrink, please, prove, or disappear?
   How does that show up in your body or your choices?

5. What part of you is ready to be seen
   for how you survived
   and for how deeply you longed to feel free?

Next Steps

Let your insight move through you and become something lived.
These are gentle invitations; choose what speaks to you.

- Choose one survival identity that feels
  most present right now,
  or choose all the ones that apply.
  Let them each teach you something.
- Spend a few days noticing your patterns:
  When does this identity show up?
  What does it protect you from?
  What does it cost you?
- If none of the identities feel like yours,
  name and describe your own.
  Let your language be a mirror:
  honest, intuitive, yours.
- Write a letter to one version of yourself
  who learned to survive in this way.
  Thank them.
  Reassure them.
  Invite them to rest.
- Begin a "What I'm Ready to Release" list.
  Add to it gently.
  You don't need urgency, just awareness.

Integration

This work is not an exercise in abandoning the past;
it's about understanding that past so you can move forward with clarity
and care.

You didn't choose the wounds.
But you get to choose the healing.
You are allowed to grow beyond the roles that once kept you safe.
You are allowed to belong to yourself now.
There's no need to rush;
approach your healing gently,
intentionally,
one truth at a time.

CHAPTER 3

From Chaos to Grace

*"Instead of spreading pain, you chose to heal. Not just once, but over
and over. That's courage."*
—Rainier Wylde

Where We've Been, Where We're Going

In Chapter 2,
we explored the roles we adopted to survive,
the identities shaped by our need for safety, love, and belonging.

Now, we go deeper into the environments that shaped those roles.
Beyond what we did to survive,
we explore *why* we had to.

In this chapter, we'll explore the impact of chaotic and emotionally
unsafe early environments:
how they affect the developing nervous system, disrupt attachment,
and interrupt the natural stages of identity formation.

We'll begin to understand how chronic stress rewires our
sense of safety,
why certain behaviors feel hard to change,
and how dysregulation becomes a baseline.

There's no need to place blame here.
We're simply returning to the root
so we can finally shift the patterns that no longer serve us.

This is where we begin the move from automatic survival to
conscious healing,
from chaos to grace.

The Landscape of Chaos

Imagine waking up each day
never knowing which version of your world you'll face.

Some mornings,
silence demands you walk on eggshells,
every breath measured,
every move calculated.

Other days,
the air crackles with tension,
shifting from eerily quiet to suddenly explosive.

Even calm feels temporary,
a brief pause before the next storm.

You learn to scan faces,
anticipate moods,
and read energy like second nature,
all because your safety depends on it.

You suppress your needs,
play roles,
and adapt quickly,
just to get through another day.

For those of us who grew up in unstable environments,
we don't have to imagine this at all.
Because for those living in chaos,
this isn't a phase.

It becomes the air they breathe.
Fear, unpredictability, and hypervigilance are wired into the nervous system.

On the outside,
they may appear composed, capable,
even "resilient."

But inside,
the body is bracing.
The nervous system never stops scanning.
And identity becomes entwined less with truth
and more with survival.

The Imprint of Chaos:
How It Shapes Us from the Beginning

We don't just experience chaos;
we absorb it.

It imprints on our nervous system
and rewires how we relate to ourselves, others, and the world.

From our earliest days,
chaos can shape us.

And while the specifics vary,
the impact often follows familiar threads.

Our younger selves carry the imprint of the chaos we once endured,
holding tight to the survival strategies that kept us safe.

Let's take a look at how chaos can affect us at different developmental
stages.

The Infant

A baby enters the world needing safety, stability, and consistent
nurturing.
When care is inconsistent—
sometimes loving, sometimes absent or harsh—
their nervous system learns that love is unpredictable.

Even before words,
the body braces for uncertainty.
The baby begins to move through life with vigilance,
never fully at ease,
always waiting for the next rupture.
I was worthy of tenderness from the very beginning.

The Toddler

Curiosity is meant to be encouraged
during the explorative toddler years.

But in a chaotic home,
curiosity may be punished, ignored, or met with frustration.

The toddler learns that independence comes with a cost.
They begin to shrink themselves to stay safe,
growing cautious or hyperaware.
I was never too much; my curiosity was sacred.

The Young Child

A time meant for identity and confidence
becomes an exercise in emotional management.

The child learns to scan the room,
to keep the peace.

Some children become the fixer or the quiet one.
Others overachieve, rebel, or retreat inward.

Different strategies,
same deeper story:
*I had to become someone else to feel safe, but I never stopped longing to
be me.*

The Preadolescent

As self-worth begins to seek external reflection,
the child discovers that validation is conditional.

Love is earned through performance.
Praise is inconsistent.

They may start to dissociate or withdraw.
I learned to perform for love, but I was already enough.

The Adolescent

In the season of independence and identity,
chaos makes trust feel dangerous.

Some teens rebel,
others shut down,
and many become people-pleasers, overachievers, or perfectionists,
trying to earn safety through control.

Relationships feel both essential and risky.
Teens crave belonging
but fear rejection, abandonment, or betrayal.
So they second-guess their instincts,
hide their emotions,
or overfunction to stay connected.

The world tells them to grow up,
but their nervous system is still fighting invisible battles.
I was doing my best to belong in a world that didn't always feel safe.

The Emerging Adult

Somewhere between adolescence and adulthood,
a new kind of tension begins to stir.

Emerging adults long for freedom but fear what it might cost.
They may leave home, physically or emotionally,
but the old dynamics follow them.

This is a season of trial and error,
of reaching for independence while still craving approval,
of stumbling through first loves, first heartbreaks, and first real
failures.

They try to prove their worth through success,
lose themselves in connection,
or shrink from the pressure of becoming someone.

The past is still close enough to echo,
but the future feels too far away to trust.
I was becoming myself while still trying to survive who I had been.

The Young Adult

By adulthood,
a person's chaos may be behind them,
but its effects linger.

Trusting themselves feels hard.
Calm feels unfamiliar, even unsafe.

Some young adults burn out from years of overfunctioning.
Others feel stuck, numb, or lost.

Survival has been the default for so long,
it's hard to imagine anything else.

The imprint begins to surface in relationships:
walls go up or boundaries dissolve completely.
They may choose partners who mirror the unpredictability they
grew up with,
or they may overextend, trying to keep everyone happy,
afraid of repeating what they once lived through.

Parenting can trigger unhealed wounds.
The desire to do better for their children
is often tangled with fear, guilt, or emotional exhaustion.

They love deeply.
But trusting that love is safe
takes time.
I was learning how to heal what I never asked to carry.

Chaos and the Survival State

When survival is your baseline,
there is no space for growth.

Maslow's hierarchy of needs shows this clearly:
At the foundation, we require food, shelter, and physical safety.
Only once we have these things
can we move toward love, connection, self-worth, and personal
fulfillment.

But when childhood is marked by chaos and unmet needs,
both physical and emotional,
we often become stuck at that base level.

Survival becomes the only goal.

Rather than forming a clear sense of self,
we shape-shift to maintain order.
We adopt roles:

the Driven Doer,
the Sensitive Soul,
the Heart-Centered Harmonizer,
the Lost Child,
the Quiet Seeker,
the Vivacious Visionary,
the Legacy Transformer.

These roles protect us.
They help us navigate the unpredictable.
But they also bury our true needs beneath the demands of the environment.

And over time,
we internalize a silent fear:
If I stop managing, fixing, or performing, everything might fall apart.

This isn't just psychological;
it's neurological.

Our patterns were formed from necessity,
because our brains and bodies were doing their best to protect us.

When safety was unpredictable,
our nervous system adapted.
We learned how to scan, anticipate, react, perform, and withdraw,
because we had to.

Even when the danger is long gone,
our system doesn't automatically know that.
Sometimes, safety itself can feel unfamiliar,
unsettling,
even threatening.

Stillness might trigger anxiety.
Kindness might feel suspicious.
Rest might feel like danger.

This is why healing can feel so hard:
You're asking your body to trust something
it was once trained to fear.

You can't simply think your way out of survival.
But you *can* gently rewire, relearn, and return,
one moment of safety at a time.

Simply recognizing this,
naming it,
is the beginning of the way out.

Awareness doesn't solve everything,
but it opens the door.
It lets in light.
It reassures your system,
There's another way.

The Many Faces of Chaos

Not all chaos looks the same.

Sometimes it's loud, violent, and undeniable.
Other times, it's subtle,
woven into daily life so quietly that it goes unnoticed for years.

Understanding its different forms
helps us recognize what we've absorbed
and what may still be living in us.

1. External Chaos
This is the chaos we can see,
the kind that lives outside of us.

It includes things like violence and abuse—
whether physical, emotional, verbal, psychological, sexual, or
spiritual—
addiction, financial instability,
and growing up in unsafe neighborhoods
or systems marked by injustice.

When our surroundings are unpredictable,
our bodies learn to scan for danger
and stay on guard.

Even in adulthood, even in safe places,
stability can feel unfamiliar
or strangely unsafe.

2. Relational Chaos
This form of chaos comes from inconsistent or conditional love.

It's the hot-and-cold caregiver,
the emotionally unavailable parent,
or love that's tangled in power dynamics.

It teaches us to earn connection
by being perfect,
by staying small,
or by pleasing others at the cost of ourselves.

Even in adulthood,
we may find ourselves drawn to relationships that feel like home;
unhealthy as they may be,
they at least feel familiar.

We might mistake unpredictability for passion.
We might fear speaking up,
believing love can be lost the moment we show our full selves.

3. Internal Chaos
Sometimes the noise doesn't come from outside;
it lives within.

Racing thoughts, emotional overwhelm, chronic anxiety, freeze
responses.
These often begin in childhood,
when big feelings weren't safe to express,
when we had to stay hyperaware just to get through the day.

Even when life looks calm,
even when life looks *good*,
the storm continues in the mind and body.

We seek distraction or control
because stillness feels unbearable.
Silence can echo with fear.

And so, we stay busy.
We overthink.
We micromanage emotions—ours and everyone else's.
Because our nervous system still remembers what it once took to survive.

4. Generational and Cultural Chaos
Not all chaos begins with us.

Some is inherited,
passed down through family trauma, cultural expectations, or
religious messaging that disconnects us from our truth.

We may feel an unconscious pull
to carry burdens that were never ours to begin with
or to live up to ideals that silence our authenticity.

Recognizing these layers of chaos
will help you gain clarity.

Awareness softens the grip of old patterns
and opens the door to something new.
Each layer you name
is one step closer to reclaiming your wholeness.

Pause and notice:
Which forms of chaos feel familiar to you?
What survival patterns might have once protected you
but now feel heavy to carry?

Unhealed Pain in Disguise

The chaos we experience doesn't disappear
when we grow up or leave home.
It lingers
in our bodies,
our behaviors,
and our beliefs.

This is what Carl Jung referred to as the "shadow self":
the parts of us shaped by pain, fear, shame, and unmet needs.

The shadow isn't bad;
it's simply unseen.

It holds the strategies we developed to survive
when we didn't feel safe.

And if we don't bring it into the light,
it quietly directs our lives from beneath the surface.

These parts don't scream;
they whisper.

They guide our habits,
influence our reactions,
and shape our relationships
in ways we don't always recognize.

But the shadow is a messenger.

And when we listen to it with compassion,
it shows us the places where healing is ready to begin.

Potential Shadow Selves

The chaos we lived through shaped our environment,
and by extension, how we learned to be.

To protect ourselves,
we developed patterns that once kept us safe
but now keep us stuck.

These patterns often show up in subtle, shadowed ways:
perfectionism, people-pleasing, emotional avoidance, or self-isolation.

What often get labeled as character flaws
are actually survival strategies.

And the first step in shifting them
is learning to see them clearly—without shame.

Perfectionism: The Fear of Not Being Enough

Perfectionism is more than striving for excellence;
it's a way to feel safe in a world that once felt chaotic.

When love or approval was conditional,
perfection became protection.

You overwork.
You overprepare.
You fear that one mistake could unravel everything.

Rest feels threatening.
Validation becomes a lifeline.
Perfection offers a sense of control,
a way to stay one step ahead of disappointment or disapproval.

But the cost is high:
It often delivers shame,
as well as burnout, anxiety, chronic self-doubt,
and a life lived on high alert.

You begin to forget who you are
beneath all the effort.

People-Pleasing:
The Loss of Authenticity
for Acceptance

In a home where emotions were unstable,
we learned that peace depended on keeping others happy.
So we tuned in to everyone else's needs
and tuned out our own.

You say yes when you mean no.
You avoid conflict.
You apologize for simply existing.
You become whatever someone needs you to be
because it feels safer than being yourself.

And for a time, it was.
It helped you stay connected,
avoid punishment,
and minimize tension.
It may have even kept you emotionally or physically safe.

But the cost of that safety was your voice,
your needs,
your sense of self.

Over time, this shape-shifting leaves you disconnected from your
own truth,
unsure where others end and you begin.

Avoidance: The Hidden Fear of Emotional Pain

Sometimes the overwhelm was too much.
Shutting down was the only way to cope.

You check out.
You numb with busyness, scrolling, or sleep.

You avoid intimacy, hard conversations,
or anything that asks you to feel.

Avoidance doesn't mean you don't care.
It means your nervous system is trying to protect you from feeling
too much.

But what's buried
will always find its way back up,
asking to be witnessed.

Hyper-Independence:
The Fear of Relying on Others

When trust was broken early,
dependence became dangerous.

You stopped asking,
stopped needing,
stopped hoping anyone would show up.

You pride yourself on doing it all alone.
You don't let people in, even when you're drowning.

But beneath the self-sufficiency is grief:
the kind that longs for safe connection
but doesn't know how to receive it.

Pause and notice:
Which of these patterns feel familiar to you?
What might they have been protecting?
What are they still costing you?

The Shadow as a Guide, Not a Threat

The shadow isn't something to banish;
it's something to welcome home.

It holds the younger versions of you
who had to survive what you never should've had to endure.

It carries unmet needs
and unspoken stories.

And when you meet those parts of you with curiosity instead of
criticism,
everything begins to shift.

Ask yourself,

>*What is this part of me trying to protect?*
>*What truth or feeling have I pushed away?*
>*What would happen if I met it with grace instead of judgment?*

This is the beginning of wholeness:
acknowledging the pain
and remembering who you've always been underneath it.

Surviving the Storm

From the very beginning,
movement was my first language,
the way my energy found its way into the world before I ever had
words for it.

There was an urgency in me,
a boundless, electric force
that felt too big for my parents to hold.

My mom, though active herself,
didn't quite know what to do with it.
I'm sure my energy reflected something back to her:
perhaps it was a mirror of her own intensity,
a reminder of what she had to suppress long ago.
I imagine it stirred her nervous system,
exacerbated her own dysregulation.
She wasn't trying to shut me down.
She just didn't know how to hold what hadn't been held in her.

When my parents couldn't contain my energy,
they sent me outside to run it off.

I never saw it as punishment.
I loved the rhythm of my feet against the earth,
the way my body felt fully alive in motion.

But when my energy was inconvenient,
it became something to manage.

If I fidgeted too much in the car,
they'd pull over and make me run beside it.

At first, I didn't think of it as punishment.
I made it fun when I could,
because I always tried to make the best of things.
It's who I've always been:
the one who turns pain into play,
the one who carries joy, even through the weight.

But some days, it stung.
Some days, I felt humiliated,
ashamed,
like I was too much for the people around me:
too loud, too alive,
too full of energy for anyone to hold with kindness.

My instincts should have been nurtured.
Instead, they were managed,
controlled,
tamed.

And slowly, I learned to disappear,
to shrink,
to survive.

Can you imagine what it does to a child
to suppress their natural exuberance?
Where does that energy go?
What does it become?

It wasn't just disappearing that kept me safe.
There was also nature:
steady, sacred, and wild like me.
It gave me something my early environment couldn't:
a place where I didn't have to be small to be loved.

Nature never tried to tame me.
It welcomed me.

The whisper of wind in the trees,
the rush of river over rock,
the still presence of ancient oaks—
these became my constants,
my sanctuary.

I found belonging and joy in the steadiness of the earth beneath me,
in the sky above.

My pockets were always full of the day's best treasures:
rocks, pinecones, bits of bark.
They were proof that some things stayed steady,
no matter how much I moved.

In nature, I didn't have to be less.
I didn't have to shrink.
I could run, feel, breathe...
and still belong.

Long before I had the words for it,
my body knew what safety felt like.
My energy, my soul, and my nervous system
were already co-regulating with the earth,

already learning that not everything had to be braced against,
that some places could hold me, just as I was.

And beyond all of that,
my deepest refuge was my connection to God and the angels.
Even as a child, I felt their presence.
I didn't just believe; I *knew*.
They were with me in the quiet,
holding me when the world felt unstable.

I waited every night for my angel to rest on my legs.
It was then—and only then—
that I felt safe enough to fall asleep.

Movement.
Nature.
The Divine.

These were my lifelines.
They carried me then.
They carry me still.

When I lost access to what kept me grounded—
when I couldn't move freely,
when nature was out of reach,
when I questioned whether God had abandoned me—
my body reacted.

Sometimes, the only movement I engaged in was walking home from
the bus stop,
up a mountain road with a heavy backpack and a heavier heart.
Sometimes, it was running laps around the house

just to burn off the excess that no one knew what to do with.
I wasn't being playful
or creative.
My movement was reduced to management.

There were so many things that got in the way:
weather, family dynamics, homework, chores,
tending to everyone else's needs.

And when I couldn't move, couldn't reach for the trees or the sky,
when I couldn't feel God...
I tensed.
I spiraled.
I searched for anything to hold on to.
Disconnection didn't just affect my mind;
it rattled my entire being.

But those lifelines never really left me.
They are part of me,
sacred threads woven into the fabric of who I am.

No matter what has changed,
they remain.
And they've always led me back to myself.

But Home Was a Different World Altogether

I was born into an abusive environment,
one marked by fear, control, and volatility.
My parents, both burdened by their own unhealed trauma and
mental illness,
created a household that felt more like a battlefield than a sanctuary.

From my earliest memories, I understood that love was conditional,
that safety was fragile,
that approval could be taken as quickly as it was given.

Like many children of chaos,
I adapted by becoming what my environment demanded.

I adopted all the previously mentioned archetypes:

I was the Driven Doer,
believing that if I excelled,
if I was good enough,
I could finally earn the love and stability I longed for.
I cleaned obsessively
and organized everything I could.
Because if I kept things just right,
maybe nothing would explode.
Maybe no one would get hurt.
My safety lay in control,
over both my space
and how I showed up in the world.

I was the Sensitive Soul,
absorbing everyone's unspoken pain
long before it was ever named.
I could feel what wasn't being said:
the rage behind a forced smile,
the tension in a silent room.
I learned to read tone, posture, and mood
with the precision of someone who had no choice.

I felt everything
too much, too soon, too often:
the chaos,
the violence,
the fear that never fully left the air.

My empathy was my superpower...
and my greatest exhaustion.
Because no one asked if I was okay.
They just kept handing me their pain,
and I kept holding it,
hoping that maybe, if I could carry enough,
someone would finally feel safe.
And then maybe I would, too.

I was the Heart-Centered Harmonizer,
soothing tension, keeping the peace.
Living with two parents navigating their own mental illness and
emotional instability,
I became the buffer,
the stabilizer,
the one who tried to calm the storm before it broke.

I knew how to sense a shift in the room before a single word was spoken,
and I learned to shape myself around it.
If I could keep things light, quiet, and agreeable,
maybe I could keep things safe.

I was the Lost Child,
fading into the background,
trying to become invisible when things felt too loud, too unsafe.
If I didn't ask for much,
maybe I wouldn't make things worse.

I was the Quiet Seeker,
always watching, always wondering.
I retreated inward when the world felt too loud.
I wanted to hide,
but also to search for something deeper.
I built a rich inner world
because the outer one rarely made sense.
Silence became my protection and portal.

I was the Vivacious Visionary,
full of possibility,
always dreaming of something more.

I was the Legacy Transformer,
even then,
knowing in my bones
this could not continue with me.

Each adaptation became a thread in the tapestry of my survival.
Each part of me carried pain,
but also the deep, aching hope that life could someday be different.

The God I Knew vs. the God They Preached

Religion, like love, was a double-edged sword.
More than once, between the ages of eight and thirteen,
I was ordered to stand alone in a prayer line
to be "delivered from fear."

In case you're unfamiliar, this meant being called to the front of the
church
while others looked on
so that hands could be laid on me,
prayers spoken,
and the fear inside me, or the headaches, prayed away in Jesus' name.
These prayers were not gentle or quiet;
they were delivered with spiritual urgency.

Why? Because I was timid,
quiet,
shy.
Because I had chronic headaches
and rarely spoke unless spoken to.
Because I flinched at raised voices
and cried easily.

My parents didn't recognize these as signs of anxiety.
To them, these were signs that something was spiritually wrong,
that fear itself had taken hold of me.
And they believed I needed deliverance.

Most of the time, it was my mom who sent me.
And I obeyed.
Because I didn't want to get in trouble—

and because somewhere inside,
I hoped maybe God would meet me there.

But the God they believed in
and the God I felt in my bones
often felt like two different beings.
And that got confusing.

Standing there—small, exposed, unsure—
I felt like the ultimate failure.
No matter how hard I tried to be everything to everyone—
to be invisible, compliant, easy—
fear still leaked out of me.
And to my parents, that meant something in me needed to
be cast out.

What I needed was safety, reassurance, and connection.
What I received was public exposure and shame.

One time, after a visiting speaker led a service on casting out demons,
my parents brought that message home, literally.
They sat me down and staged their own "deliverance" session.

They didn't speak gently.
They directed me, aggressively,
to cry, cough, yawn,
do *something* to prove the demon was leaving my body.

I was a child,
already afraid.
And, reflecting, I wonder,
Did they not see that I was afraid because of them?

These weren't isolated incidents, either.
They were part of a pattern,
one that wrapped spiritual language around emotional and
psychological control.
It left me confused
and unprotected.
I was terrified,
not of demons,
but of the very people who claimed they were saving me.

I was exposed to many forms of Christianity:
Moravian, Baptist, Episcopal, Methodist, Lutheran,
nondenominational, and more.
My parents were seekers, curious about belief systems,
drawn to information and theological ideas.
But they never stayed long.
They struggled to connect with people
and avoided accountability,
likely because of everything happening at home.
The instability extended beyond our house;
it followed us into every church.

The very places that should have taught unconditional love
instead taught me to measure my value through effort, silence, and
sacrifice.

I was praised for being quiet,
for not questioning adults,
for taking care of others without complaint.
I learned that good behavior meant swallowing hard feelings
and pushing through pain without making a scene.

I learned that obedience mattered more than honesty
and that pleasing others was more important than protecting myself.

I internalized the belief that love was earned
through compliance, performance, and spiritual submission.
I had to earn love from my family,
and even from God.

It wasn't just my parents who failed us, either;
the betrayal extended to the churches.
Pastors, elders, and trusted members
saw the emotional bruises,
the fear in our eyes,
the way we walked on eggshells.
They heard the whispers.
They knew.
And they did nothing.

They chose silence over truth,
comfort over courage.

How could someone claim to love God
and ignore suffering in plain sight?
How could they preach justice and mercy,
yet look away when children were being harmed?

These are questions I still carry.

I've already begun that work,
the slow, sacred process of making peace.
I don't do it for them;

I do it for me.
Because I deserve peace.

Forgiveness used to feel like a command,
something I was expected to do quickly, cleanly, and completely.
I thought it meant pretending everything was okay
or opening myself back up to people who had harmed me.

But I've come to understand forgiveness differently.
It doesn't mean excusing the harm
or seeking reconciliation.
It's a personal, imperfect, and sacred process,
a gift I give myself.
It's a way to release what's hurting me
so I can live with a little more freedom in my heart,
my body,
my mind.

Sometimes, forgiveness looks like remembering it wasn't about me.
Sometimes, it looks like setting boundaries
or choosing not to carry pain that doesn't belong to me.
There's no formula
or one-time decision involved.
I'm allowing peace in
and protecting it
like my life depends on it.

Because sometimes, it does.

Holding on to the weight of other people's silence
only corrodes what's sacred in me.
I choose not to let their inaction define my faith,

my future,
or my freedom.

I wasn't angry.
I just knew I would never be like them.
I saw their fear,
their complacency,
their unwillingness to disrupt their own comfort
to stand for someone else's truth.

And I vowed,
deep in my bones,
that I would not live that way.
I would not close my eyes to suffering.
I would not choose comfort over compassion.
My life would be different.

Still, I played my roles well.
I became a caretaker,
rescuing my mom from my dad's violence,
managing their emotional and mental instability,
rushing her to the hospital when she was sick,
trying to hold our fragile world together.

Even in the middle of all that pain,
something in me remained untouched.

My mom often said I had a calming presence,
that even as a child, I carried a kind of light.
She told me how

in nurseries with crying babies,
I would smile,
and the crying would stop.

Animals, too, seemed drawn to me.

That light wasn't something I created;
it was grace.
It was always present,
always holding me,
even when people failed me.

Because the truth is,
my struggle was never with God.
The problem wasn't faith itself,
but the way it was used:
twisted to control,
to manipulate,
to excuse inaction, in the church and in my family.

And yet, even as I observed and questioned people,
I never questioned God's presence.
Deep down, I knew He and the angels were with me,
even when those who claimed to serve Him turned
away—or harmed me.
And that quiet, steady, unmistakable fact
became its own form of rescue.

The Cost

The cost of my caregiving role ran deep.
I believed, at the core of me,
that if I could just save my mother,
maybe everything else would be okay.

I believed I could save her
from my father's volatility,
from her own unraveling,
from the pain that lived just beneath the surface.

I thought that if I could keep her physically healthy,
emotionally stable,
and mentally calm,
then maybe she'd be all right.
And maybe I would be, too.

If I could keep her at peace,
keep her close,
keep her from falling apart,
then maybe I wouldn't lose her.

To my mother, I was more than a daughter;
I was the one who held her together.

I didn't have the language for trauma bonds yet,
but I lived inside one.

My mother could be warm and loving one moment
and cold, mean, or unreachable the next.

That inconsistency kept me clinging,
desperate for connection,
willing to endure pain just to feel wanted.

Later in life, she would tell me—
without acknowledging the weight of it—
that she had made me her "substitute spouse,"
transferring her emotional needs onto me.

The weight of that role was suffocating.
And honestly, it felt violating.

But it was all I knew how to do.

And that desire to save through sacrifice didn't stay confined to my
childhood or to our home.
It became a pattern
I carried into every relationship,
even long after the danger had passed.

I learned to sacrifice myself for the well-being of others.
I mistook self-abandonment for love.
I equated responsibility with worth.

I became The Lost Child:
quiet, compliant, invisible.

I faded into the background
just to feel safe.

At school, I was liked,
but not truly seen.

I smiled.
I followed the rules.
I got good grades.

But at lunch,
I often ate alone,
retreating to a kind teacher's classroom
or slipping outside to avoid the noise.

I became an expert in disappearing.

When I felt the world was too much,
I pulled inward.

I was there,
but I wasn't really there.

I learned how to make myself small,
how to float just under the radar,
how to stay out of the line of fire
by not taking up too much space.

But while I became invisible on the outside,
my body was keeping score.

By my teens, I was already living with chronic pain:
headaches that throbbed like a silent scream
and joints that ached as if they carried centuries of sorrow.

I didn't yet understand that my body was carrying
what my voice couldn't speak.

I remember being sent to stand in prayer lines at church,
over and over again.
I remember the guest pastors, the healing services, the oil on my
forehead,
the hands pressed gently on my shoulders.

I always asked for prayer
because I was told to,
and because if there was even a chance it might help,
I didn't want to miss it.
I was compliant.
I had an image to uphold.
And I was in pain.

So I asked for relief
from the fear,
from the headaches,
from the invisible weight pressing in on all sides.

I hoped someone could see what I couldn't explain,
that someone could pray it out of me.

But the pain persisted,
unacknowledged, untreated, and invisible.
Just like so many other parts of me.

And yet, through all this,
something bright in me still fought to exist.

Lifelines of My Own

At eight years old, I started babysitting a family with four kids.

By thirteen, I was cleaning houses after school,
trading childhood for responsibility.

I threw myself into academics and music.
I learned clarinet, oboe, bassoon, trombone, baritone, guitar,
percussion,
and even a little piano.

Each instrument became a new voice,
a new way to express what I couldn't yet put into words.

I performed with a mime troupe at the World's Fair in Knoxville,
where silence finally became something safe,
something sacred.

Movement, creativity, and learning
all became lifelines, too.
They were places where I felt more like me and less like a shadow.

At thirteen, I traveled to England through an exchange program.
I walked through the countryside and city streets,
navigating spaces far from home,
feeling something new rise in me:

possibility.

It was the first time I tasted freedom,
the first time I realized there was a life beyond what I'd known.

But even with all these lifelines—
the music, the motion,
the brief taste of something wider—
I wasn't free,
not yet.

I returned home from England
to the same volatility, the same roles,
the same unspoken rules that had shaped me.

Something in me had expanded,
but I didn't know how to live from that space yet,
not when survival still required shrinking.

So I tucked the freedom away
and held it close like a secret,
a quiet knowing that one day,
life could be different.

Growing Up Too Fast

By the time both of my siblings left our home for good,
I was only eight.

It wasn't an act of rebellion.
They left because the environment was unbearable.
They had run away.
The Department of Social Services got involved.
My parents said it was defiance,
but I knew it was survival.

And once my siblings were gone,
I was the one left behind
to carry what they couldn't.

That's when the weight of it all truly settled in.
With no one else to absorb my parents' intensity
or deflect their emotional chaos,
I became the landing place for everything unspoken,
unprocessed, and unhealed.
There was no buffer,
only me
and the full force of their pain.

I endured my father's rage,
as well as his silence and absence.

I managed my mother's emotional dependency,
layered with emptiness and manipulation.

I was expected to intuit their moods,
meet their needs,
and hold their pain.

I became their mirror,
their container,
their projection screen.

And it almost broke me.

There were days I felt like disappearing entirely,
days when the pain felt too big, too constant, too invisible to survive.
My thoughts whispered that maybe it would be easier if I just didn't
exist.
I never acted on them,
but I heard them.
And I believed them.

I have hated myself.
And I've been cruel—not to others, but to myself.
I've held myself to impossible standards,
berated myself for being too much or not enough.

There were moments I hit my head against walls
or punched them.
It wasn't often, but still enough to know something in me was
breaking.
And I didn't know how else to let it out.

I didn't know how to be kind to myself.
All I knew was that this was how I could survive.
But survival isn't the same as being alive.

I was barely holding on.
Day by day, I lost more of myself trying to hold together
what was never mine to carry.

By my early twenties, I hit a breaking point.
Years of suppressed anger, unresolved grief,
and relentless self-abandonment finally caught up to me.

I was exhausted, physically, emotionally, spiritually.
I had spent most of my life bracing, performing, managing,
and it was all too much.

I didn't fully understand the patterns or where they came from.
I just knew something was wrong.

I was living, but I wasn't alive.

And then my brother died.
Two months after I was married, he was killed in a
tragic motorcycle accident.

The grief was unbearable. It cracked me open.
But that loss forced me to begin confronting another one:
the loss of myself.

In my grief, I turned inward.
I turned toward healing.

I realized how long I had been disappearing,
how much of me had been hidden, managed, muted just to survive.
I couldn't pretend anymore. Something had to change.

More Than a Diagnosis

I pursued a Master's in Counseling,
seeking to understand my own pain
and, in doing so, to help others heal theirs.

Looking back now, I remember how I could relate to so many
diagnoses in the DSM:
anxiety, depression, complex trauma, grief, even dissociation.

But I was still functioning, still achieving, still pushing through.
On the outside, I seemed fine.
Inside, I was unraveling.

And yet, I rarely met the full criteria for any diagnosis.

Over time, I began to move away from the clinical model.
While it was helpful in some ways,
it didn't fully reflect my experience and truth.

I believe human experience is more than a diagnosis or two.

We do ourselves a disservice, I believe, when we *become* our anxiety or
our depression,
when we reduce ourselves to symptoms rather than listening to them
as messengers.

These patterns, these emotions,
they're not our identity.

They're information,
signals pointing to what's unhealed, what's unmet, what's asking to
be seen.

That shift, away from labels and toward self-understanding, was part
of my healing,
part of my journey of coming home to me.

My life had been shaped by chaos.
But I was choosing something else.

I was choosing grace.

The Nature of Chaos

It was terrifying at first
to stop overgiving,
to stop chasing peace
at the expense of my truth.

But I knew
if I didn't let go of those old roles,
I would continue to lose myself.

So I began to walk the path of healing,
slowly,
imperfectly,
one layer at a time.

And what I discovered was this:
I could love deeply with trauma.
But I could not love fully and wholly,
nor receive what I truly longed for,
until I learned to love myself.

The healing didn't happen all at once.
It was an ongoing process,
one that still continues to this day.
Because healing isn't a destination.
It's what unfolds
when we choose to embrace and love our true self,
over and over again.

I've come to understand
that trauma doesn't stay in the past.
It echoes.
It moves through our nervous system,
shapes our relationships,
and quietly informs how we show up in the world.

It's subtle
and hidden.
It's in the anxiety we can't shake
and the pain we can't name.
It's the self-sabotage,
the hypervigilance,
the way we never quite feel safe,
even when nothing is wrong.

The body always keeps the score.
And true healing
asks us to listen
to what the trauma has been trying to say
all along.

Did I Choose This?

I've often wrestled with the question of choice.

Was my path carved by fate,
woven by divine hands?

Or was it shaped by the circumstances I was born into
and the choices I made along the way?

And yet,
are they even choices
if we aren't conscious of the patterns driving us?

Is it free will
if we're living from survival,
from wounds,
from someone else's story?

I've come to believe that real choice begins
when we become aware,
when we remember who we are
beneath the programming.

Awareness changed everything for me.

It gave me the quiet, powerful agency to rise
and say, *This is not where my story ends.*
It helped me shape something new
out of what I learned from the past.

Chaos has always been there.

But grace has always been there, too,
a current beneath even the most turbulent waters.

Unseen,
but unmistakable.

It reminded me that even when I couldn't see the path ahead,
I wasn't lost.
I was being led.

And maybe the paradox is this:
We are both led and leading.
We are held by divine hands,
yet free to shape what we become.

So, did I choose this path?

In some ways, yes.
In others, it chose me.

But now that I have awareness,
I always get to choose.

From Fragmented to Whole

Because of this understanding,
I no longer see myself as fragmented
or broken
or loving from a wounded place,
clinging to people or patterns that only mirror my old pain.

I no longer reach for safety in places
that were never meant to hold me.
I no longer grasp for love
in ways that cost me myself.

Now, I love from wholeness,
a state I continue to nurture
with grace,
with awareness,
with truth.

I trust in ways I never could before:
trusting others,
but more than that,
trusting myself.
And trust is still a practice,
a choice I return to
over and over.

I receive love now the way it was always meant to be received:
openly and honestly.
I lead with love,
and I don't abandon myself to do it.
I let myself be fully seen in my messy, joyful, grieving, growing self.

I hold boundaries that honor my peace.
I let myself have preferences, needs, and dreams,
and I speak them out loud.
I don't shrink anymore.
I treat myself like the queen I know I am.
And that love,
the kind I give to myself first,
is what teaches others how to love me, too.

This is the movement from chaos to grace,
from fragmentation to wholeness,
from surviving to choosing.

This is healing:
not a destination,
but a lifelong unfolding,
a sacred return
to who I've always been.

Invitation

Before you begin,
pause.

Check in with your body.
Do you need a sip of water,
a breath of fresh air,
or a moment to move or stretch?

Find a quiet, grounding space.
Let it feel safe and supportive.

You aren't fixing anything.
You're only noticing what has shaped you
and meeting it with compassion.

Let this be gentle.
Let it be honest.
Let it be yours.

Reflection Prompts

There are no right answers here,
only invitations to notice what's stirring
and to witness what's asking to be seen.

Recognizing Chaos in Your Life

- Where do I feel overwhelmed, drained, or stuck?
- What areas of my life feel heavy (relationships, responsibilities, decisions, etc.)?
- In what ways am I caught in cycles of stress, perfectionism, or people-pleasing?

Identifying Survival Roles and Their Cost

- What roles have I played to maintain harmony or safety?
- How have these roles protected me? What have they cost me?
- What strengths have they offered, and where are they now limiting my peace or authenticity?

Understanding the Inner Child's Influence

- When do I feel small, anxious, or unseen, as if I'm still my younger self?
- What does that inner child long for (play, love, safety, expression, etc.)?
- How can I nurture that part of me today?

Breaking Patterns of Fear and Control

- How does fear still shape the way I show up in the world?
- Where am I gripping too tightly (trying to control, perform, or prove)?
- What would it look like to soften and let grace guide me?

Releasing and Reclaiming Myself
- What am I being called to release, surrender, or embrace?
- What hidden parts of me have I rejected out of fear or shame?
- How can I meet those parts now with gentleness?

Speaking to My Younger Self
- If my teenage self still feels unseen, what do they need to hear today?
- What words would make them feel safe, valued, and free?

You can journal these reflections.
Say them out loud.
Whisper them to the parts of you still aching to be held.
Let your words become your practice:
a letter, a mirror note,
a new language of self-love.

This is how remembering becomes re-parenting.
This is how you offer the love you once needed,
right here, right now.

Next Steps

Let your insights take root through simple, embodied action.

- Choose one area of chaos, internal or external, and bring presence to it.
  What is one small step that might bring more peace, clarity, or spaciousness?
- Identify a survival role you've been living in.
  Ask, What would it feel like to lay it down, even just for today?
- Create a grounding practice to support your inner child.
  It might be journaling, walking, art, music, or something playful and freeing.
  Let it be intuitive.
- Write a short message to your younger self.
  Make it something you can return to in moments of doubt or pain.
  Post it somewhere you'll see it.
- Make a "Release and Receive" list:
  On one side, name what you're letting go of.
  On the other, name what you're choosing to welcome in its place.

Remember: None of this needs to be perfect.
Even one small step is sacred.

Integration

Take a breath and honor how far you've come,
even if all you've done is pause and notice.

You don't have to carry
what was never yours to hold.

You are allowed to set it down,
to loosen your grip,
to choose peace instead of proving.

You are not lost.
You are remembering.

And with each small shift,
you're returning to yourself.
There is grace in this unraveling.
There is strength in your softness.
There is wisdom in the slowing down.

You are being guided
through every layer of becoming,
held, seen, and loved,
even in the quiet.

Trust this release.
It's making space
for something new to rise.

CHAPTER 4

Embracing Graceful Resilience

*"Out of suffering have emerged the strongest souls; the most massive
characters are seared with scars."*
—Kahlil Gibran

Where We've Been, Where We're Going

In Chapter 3, we explored how chaos imprints itself
on the nervous system, in the roles we take on,
and in the ways we move through the world.

Survival taught us to overfunction, to stay silent, to strive for
peace at any cost.
These patterns may have once kept us safe,
but they can also keep us small.

You began to recognize where you've been reacting instead
of choosing,
surviving instead of living.

But awareness is only the beginning.

True healing asks us to go further,
to soften what was hardened,
to hold what was hidden,
to rebuild from the inside out.

This is where the practice of graceful resilience begins.

The Power of Soft Strength

We often think of resilience as pushing through:
gritting our teeth, muscling forward, carrying the weight
without breaking.

But real resilience, the kind that heals and transforms,
is something deeper.

You don't need to force anything
or pretend everything is fine.
Resilience is about learning how to bend without breaking.

Graceful resilience invites a new kind of strength,
one that includes softness.

It's the ability to meet life's challenges with both courage
and compassion,
to stay rooted when the wind blows,
and to trust your capacity, even in the unknown.

Rebuilding from Within

This chapter is about rebuilding.
You will learn how to choose wholeness over performance,
nervous system regulation over reactivity,
trust over fear.

Graceful resilience doesn't mean the absence of pain.
It means being with pain...without becoming it.

It doesn't ask for perfection, only presence,
being more connected to yourself as you move forward.

Here, we'll explore

- what graceful resilience really is and how it redefines strength;
- how to support your nervous system as you shift from survival into steady empowerment;
- why protecting your energy doesn't require closing your heart; and
- how to build resilience through practices that honor your capacity, boundaries, and needs.

You already have the courage to face the chaos.
Now, you can begin to build what comes next:
something rooted, resilient, and real.

When My Body Begged to Be Heard

Before I was able to conceive, I faced the challenge of long-term endometriosis,
a condition that brought excruciating and often debilitating pain,
the kind of pain that makes it hard to think,
to function,
to be.

Rest was never an option,
not in the world I had been raised in,
not in the patterns I had learned to live by.

I had internalized a belief I didn't yet have words for:
You push through.
You don't ask.
You don't stop.
You just keep going.

Based on the clues and cues I observed and took in,
I believe my mother likely dealt with endometriosis herself,
but we never talked about it.

In our home, the body was only discussed in terms of appearance or weight,
and even then, usually with judgment.

So I endured in silence,
feeling shame over a pain I couldn't explain
and a body I couldn't trust.

Somewhere deep within me,
a core belief was being solidified:
Your pain is yours to carry alone.
No one said it outright;
that message lived in the silence.

At the time, I couldn't see how profoundly I was abandoning myself
physically,
emotionally,
energetically.

Constantly pushing through made me look resilient and capable.
But I didn't yet know
it would cost me more than I realized.

All I knew was that I longed to be a mother,
to create the family I had always dreamed of.
I wanted to build something different,
something safe.

After seven years of marriage and a surgery
to remove the scar tissue that endometriosis had left behind,
I was finally able to conceive.

The dream of motherhood became real.
And when my first daughter was born,
it was everything I had hoped for.

She was light and delight, wonder and joy.
We read together,
explored together,
soaked up life together.

Those early days were beautiful and bonding.
And even though I was navigating so much alone,
I truly treasured the connection we shared.

But beneath the sweetness, my body was breaking down.

Just three months postpartum,
I developed a thyroid goiter,
a loud signal from within
that I needed care,
rest,
and support.

And I wanted those things, desperately.

But I was carrying decades of conditioning:
that life was supposed to be hard,
that I had to do it all myself,
that asking for help meant I was weak or failing.

There was concern from afar—
from my mom, from my sister—
but day to day,
I was on my own.

Caring for a newborn.
Managing the house.
Tending to two pets.
Trying to hold together a marriage
in which I didn't feel fully seen or supported.

I was still living the pattern:
useful,
capable,
invisible.

Yet I wanted more:
more support,
more love,
more partnership,
more health,
more space to breathe.

But I was stuck,
trapped between longing and old beliefs,
between knowing what I needed
and not believing I was allowed to have it.

So I kept going,
smiling,
functioning,
looking fine from the outside,
all while something inside me quietly unraveled.

I had spent a lifetime overriding my needs.
And this time was no different.

At eight weeks postpartum,
my then husband took a job that kept him away
for most of the next year.

And while that added to the logistical strain,
it didn't feel all that different from when he was home.

Part of me was stressed,
the part that still wanted it to work,
the part that believed relationships took communication,
effort,
and commitment.

I wanted a partner.
I wanted connection.

But another part of me
felt a strange relief.

Without the daily tension,
without the weight of being unseen pressed so close,
something in me exhaled.

I didn't have to brace for disappointment.
I didn't have to try so hard to be okay.

I could just...function.

Not happily, not fully,
but without the constant ache
of trying to make something
that wasn't working...work.

Yes, there was so much joy.
But there was also deep depletion.

I did what I had always done:
held it together,
played the caregiver,
pushed forward,
abandoned myself.

I didn't recognize yet that this wasn't just motherhood.
It was another storm I was weathering alone,
without support,
without rest,
without grace.

Loss, Isolation, and Deepening Beliefs

Between the births of my first and second daughters,
I experienced a miscarriage.

The grief was deep and quiet,
an ache that lived inside my body and my heart.

I was terrified by the bleeding,
unsure of what was normal,
unsure of what to do.

I had grown so accustomed to heavy pain,
both physical and emotional,
that I didn't know how to sound the alarm.

Even when something felt extreme,
unbearable,
not okay,
I minimized it.

I downplayed my own needs,
even in loss.

I kept moving.
Because that's what I had always done.

But looking back, I see it clearly:
I felt completely alone.

And more than that,
I believed I was supposed to be alone.

The pain of miscarriage was compounded
by an old belief I had unknowingly carried since childhood:
I am not supported.

And because that belief had shaped so many of my early experiences,
it became the lens through which I interpreted this one.
There were people on the edges of my life,
but no one really with me.
I felt invisible,
alone in my body,
alone in my grief,
alone in my need.

Even in my marriage,
I didn't feel supported.
We weren't connected.
We weren't a team.
And while I didn't have the words for it then,
I felt as alone inside the relationship
as I did outside of it.
As Gabor Maté wrote:

"The greatest damage done by neglect, trauma, or emotional loss
is not the immediate pain they inflict
but the long-term distortions they induce
in the way a developing child will continue to interpret the world
and her situation in it.
All too often these ill-conditioned implicit beliefs become self-
fulfilling prophecies in our lives."[2]

---

2 Gabor Maté, *In the Realm of Hungry Ghosts: Close Encounters with Addiction* (Berkeley, CA: North Atlantic Books, 2010), 33.

That's exactly what was happening.

I was shaping my life around a story that said
support wasn't safe,
help wouldn't come,
and my pain wasn't important.

That story wasn't born in adulthood;
it was a survival script written long before I had the words for it.

The Breaking Point:
When My Body Couldn't Go On

When I became pregnant with my second daughter,
I felt deeply grateful to have another chance to bring life into the
world.

But just ten days after her birth,
my body went into full crisis.

I developed bilateral mastitis,
a severe infection that would last not just days or weeks
but more than five months.

It was excruciating.
At times, it was life-threatening, according to my doctor.

I suffered fevers,
swelling,
pain that made functioning for myself—
let alone caring for my newborn and three-year-old—
incredibly challenging.

As if that weren't enough,
I was also battling persistent candida infections from antibiotics,
which brought brain fog, exhaustion, and overwhelming discomfort.

My weight dropped into the 80s—
dangerously low.

I was beyond depleted;
I was barely holding on.

And still,
I did the cooking,
the laundry,
the basic cleaning.
I nursed the baby,
interacted with my three-year-old,
tended to the home.
I even paid the bills.
I made sure everyone's needs were met,
including my own,
as best I could.

My mother helped when she could,
and when I had the energy,
I drove across the state with a fever
just to have some support.
But she lived far away,
and the help came in short, complicated windows.

I was parenting alone.
Even in partnership,
I was on my own.

And still,
I tried to do it all.
Still,
I tried to be everything.

Looking back now,
I can see how deeply my body was speaking,
how it was holding what I couldn't yet name.

As Inna Segal writes in *The Secret Language of Your Body*, mastitis reflects

"feeling frozen, helpless, abandoned, and unsupported...
bound by responsibilities and expectations.
Pushing away your feelings,
self-neglect, and self-sacrifice."[3]

Every word of this rings true.
My body had been carrying the weight of survival for too long,
and now it was demanding to be heard.

For years,
I had overridden my body's signals.
I had pushed through pain,
and dismissed exhaustion.
I had fawned instead of feeling,
frozen instead of speaking.

Even as my body was fighting for survival,
I still believed I needed to keep giving,
keep proving,
keep holding it all together.

But my body couldn't keep going.
And deep down,
I knew I couldn't, either.

---

3 Inna Segal, *The Secret Language of Your Body: The Essential Guide to Health and Wellness* (Carlsbad, CA: Hay House, 2009).

One night,
I found myself in the thick of it:
high fever, searing pain,
my body trembling from exhaustion.

I was trying to nurse my newborn through the fever,
trying to soothe her
and survive myself.

And I needed help.

That wasn't something I often allowed myself to need,
let alone ask for.

But that night,
I called out to my husband.

When he finally awoke from me calling him,
his sharp, cold response made it clear
he was neither willing nor able
to be available for me or our child.

And in that moment,
sweating, aching, struggling to stay upright,
something inside me shifted.

I saw the truth clearly,
maybe for the first time:

I had been waiting for someone to choose me who never would.
I had been hoping that if I gave enough,
held enough,
endured enough,
things would change.

But there,
in that moment of fever and clarity,
I knew:

I didn't need to keep proving my worth.
I didn't need someone else to save me.

I could and would choose myself.

That night wasn't just the beginning of my physical healing.
It was the moment I stopped outsourcing my value.
It was the moment I started listening to the voice I had long silenced.
It was another deeper layer of coming home to myself.

Reclaiming My Strength, One Choice at a Time

As my body continued to weaken,
my parents stepped in and helped me access nutritional intravenous
treatments.

These IVs became a lifeline,
slowly rebuilding what had been depleted over months of crisis.

With each treatment,
I felt flickers of strength returning.

But it wasn't just physical healing I needed;
it was the unraveling of old narratives:

You can't stop.
You shouldn't need.
It's your job to hold it all together.

I had to face the truth that my body had been shouting for months:
This way is no longer sustainable.

One of the hardest choices I made was to stop breastfeeding.

After nursing my first daughter for a year,
I had every intention of doing the same with my second.

But my body was begging for relief.
It simply couldn't continue.

Letting go of that expectation felt like another loss,
another thing I couldn't carry.

But deep down,
I knew it was an act of self-preservation—
and maybe, finally, self-love.

As I slowly began to regain strength and clarity,
I started to see my life through a different lens.

And with that clarity came another truth I could no longer ignore:
I had to leave my marriage.

It wasn't a rash decision.
It was the culmination of years of self-abandonment, exhaustion,
and unmet needs.

I had spent so long hoping things would change
if I just gave more,
if I was good enough,
patient enough,
quiet enough.

But I could feel something rising in me that I hadn't felt in a long
time:
certainty.

It was the kind of certainty that says,
Peace doesn't require permission.
Your well-being is reason enough.
You can walk away and still hold your head high.

I wasn't even angry.
I was just...done.

Done minimizing.
Done waiting.
Done betraying myself for someone else's comfort.

I knew I deserved more.
And so did my daughters.

I didn't do everything perfectly.
I simply did the best I could
with what I knew then.

And that was enough.

Releasing the Weight of Perception

As I moved forward,
I began to make peace with something that used to keep me tangled:

the fact that not everyone would understand my choices.

People will hold different versions of me in their minds
based on their lens, their wounds, their comfort, or their denial.

And I have no control over that.

For a long time,
I tried to explain,
to justify,
to make it make sense to people who were never meant to hold the
full truth.

But eventually,
I stopped needing to be understood.

I stopped needing to defend what I knew
in my body,
in my spirit,
in my gut.

The only thing that mattered
was that I understood.
I knew my truth,
and I was living in alignment with it.

And that became the new goal:
to stop trying to be seen clearly by everyone else
and start seeing myself clearly.

I needed to live in integrity with my own inner wisdom
and stop shrinking to fit someone else's narrative of me.

Even as I left their father,
I held on to hope that he and our daughters might build something
in the future:
a relationship rooted in care, consistency, and connection.

I knew I couldn't create that for them.
It wasn't something I could control,
neither while we were together
nor after we separated
or through the years that followed.
It would be his to cultivate,
if and when he chose to show up in that way.

But not everyone around me understood.

While I was still sick and barely holding on,
someone from the church said to me,
"You do know God hates divorce, right?"

Their words stung,
but in that moment,
I understood something even deeper:

Healing requires a change in environment.
And the first environment I had to heal
was the one I had built around self-denial.

A New Definition of Strength

Watching my daughters grow
has deepened my understanding of what strength truly is.

It doesn't mean pushing through no matter the cost,
but knowing when to stay
and when to walk away.

It listens,
softens,
and rises again.

My girls have taught me more than I could ever teach them.

Through them, I've learned

- what real love feels like: safe, soft, enduring.
- that vulnerability is not weakness; it's connection.
- that my voice matters, and it's worth using, even when it shakes.
- that asking for what I need is not selfish, but sacred.

This journey was brutal in many ways.
It brought me to my knees.
But it also brought me back to life.

It forced me to face old fears,
to release inherited patterns,
and to build a life that finally felt aligned with who I am,
not who I had been trained to be.

And maybe most importantly, it reminded me of this truth:

My strength is not measured by what I can endure.
It's measured by how willing I am
to let go of what I no longer need to carry.

It's how willing I am to heal,
to evolve,
and to create something better:
a life that feels nourishing, honest, and whole,
a life more rooted in love than survival.

This was something I had always longed for
but now could finally give to myself and my children.

I no longer brace for every gust.
I bend.
I listen.
I move with what life brings
instead of against it.
It's not always easy,
but I've learned that softening
is sometimes the bravest thing we can do.

Becoming the Woman I Am Today

This journey, brutal as it was,
shaped me into the woman I am today.

A woman who
- fully embraces self-love,
- recognizes her inherent worth,
- sets boundaries with clarity and compassion, and
- knows when to walk away from
  anything that diminishes her.

But don't mistake this for a tidy arrival point.
There wasn't one moment when everything fell into place
and I never struggled again.

This evolution was simply another layer of my becoming,
another shedding,
another return.

It was another deeper truth saying,
You are allowed to choose yourself.

There will always be more to heal,
more to uncover,
more to hold with grace.

But I no longer move from fear.
I no longer chase love or silence my truth.

I live aligned.
And I let that be enough.

The Heart of Graceful Resilience

Imagine standing in the middle of a storm.
The sky darkens.
The wind howls.
Rain lashes against your skin.
The ground beneath you shifts and trembles.

Every instinct screams,
Brace, push, fight.

But the harder you resist,
the more you're worn down.

You're exhausted.
Your breath is shallow.
Doubt and fear swirl louder than your own voice.

And still,
the storm rages on.

Then something shifts.

You realize something:
You can't stop the storm.
You can't will the winds to calm or the sky to clear.

But you can choose how you stand inside it.

Instead of stiffening,
you adjust.
You root your feet.
You soften your shoulders.
You allow yourself to sway with the wind instead of against it.

And in that moment,
you feel something new:
beyond the storm's force
is the quiet power within you.

You realize that survival requires more than resisting the storm.
You must also remember your own steadiness within it.

This is graceful resilience.

You don't need to deny your fear,
pretend you're fine, or push beyond capacity.

You can honor your limits without collapsing.
You can move with the storm without moving against yourself.

Know when to pause,
when to persist,
and when to let go.

For me, resilience wasn't gritting my teeth
and forcing myself to stay in a marriage that wasn't working.
It was finding the courage to leave.

I didn't have to cling to breastfeeding
that was painful and depleting.
It took me months to let go.
There was grief.
But eventually, I saw the truth:
that choosing to stop
was an act of care for both my daughter and myself.

Invitation

Before diving into the practices that follow,
pause.
Find a quiet, comfortable space where you feel safe and unhurried.
Maybe it's a cozy chair, a sunlit corner, or a spot outside where the
air feels grounding.

Let yourself arrive fully.
Notice how your body feels without trying to fix or change anything.
There's no rush.

Resilience begins here,
in the small, sacred act of choosing to slow down.

Grab a journal and pen or open your laptop, whatever helps you
tune in to your thoughts, feelings, and energy.
Take a slow, intentional breath.
Again, let yourself arrive in this moment.

Set aside the need for perfect insights or polished answers.
Forget about achievement.
Instead, give yourself the gift of reflection and listen for what lives
beneath the surface.

As you move through the following exercises,
bring an open heart and gentle curiosity.
Let your responses flow, without overthinking, without editing.
If emotions arise, let them.
If resistance shows up, simply notice it.
There's no need to force clarity.
Sometimes, simply sitting with the questions is more than enough.

You don't have to do this all at once.
Give yourself permission to go slow,
to pause,
to return when it feels right.

Healing and self-discovery unfold in layers,
at their own pace,
in their own time.

What feels true today might shift tomorrow.
Honor that.
Let your journey be uniquely yours.

Reflection Prompts

Embracing Vulnerability and Self-Compassion
- What physical sensations do I notice when I allow myself to fully feel?
- What happens when I trust my emotions instead of resisting them?

Releasing Old Patterns
- What belief have I been holding that might be limiting me?
- How can I rewrite it in a way that supports my healing?

Protecting Your Energy and Setting Boundaries
- How does it feel when I honor my limits without guilt?
- What is one way I can protect or share my energy today?

Cultivating Flexibility and Nervous System Trust
- Where in my life can I invite more openness and trust?
- How does my body feel when I choose flexibility instead of resistance?

Leaning on Support
- Who feels safe in my nervous system?
- What support am I ready to receive?

Final Reflections
- What practice from this chapter speaks most deeply to me today?
- What would it mean to let that one small step be enough?

Next Steps

Honor Your Body's Needs
At any point, if you need to pause, stretch, move, hydrate, rest, or nourish yourself, please do.
Your body is the home you will inhabit for a lifetime.
How you care for it today shapes your vitality, clarity, and resilience tomorrow.

Every sip of water,
every nourishing meal,
every moment of rest
is an act of gratitude for the body that carries you.

You are not here to push through introspection.
You are here to be supported in it.
Tending to your physical needs is part of the healing.

If stillness feels difficult, begin with gentle movement:
- Take a slow walk outside.
- Stretch or follow your body's intuitive rhythm.
- Dance to a song that makes you feel grounded or free.

Let movement be an act of connection, a way to tend to your nervous system and clear space for reflection.

Integration

Take a breath.
Let your shoulders drop.
Feel your feet on the ground,
your body in space,
your spirit gently returning home.

You've just walked through a powerful reminder:
Strength doesn't always roar.
Sometimes it's the whisper that says,
Rest now.
Begin again.

You don't have to hold it all.
You are allowed to protect your peace,
to honor your limits,
and to choose softness—without losing your power.

You are learning to trust yourself again.
This is graceful resilience.
And it lives in you.

CHAPTER 5

Grace Under Pressure

"The wound is the place where the Light enters you."
—Rumi

Where We've Been, Where We're Going

In Chapter 4,
we redefined resilience
from pushing through at all costs
to meeting life with presence, softness, and strength.

We explored how graceful resilience allows us to honor our limits,
support our nervous system,
and respond to life with intention rather than reaction.

There's no need for striving
or performative strength.
You must return to yourself with compassion,
especially when the storm is still swirling.

Before you move forward,
take a moment to notice how you're feeling
in your thoughts,
your body,
your energy,
and your breath.

There is no rush.
You don't have to push through just to get through.
Honor your pace.
Honor your capacity.

If you feel grounded, curious, or even gently drawn forward,
this chapter is here to meet you.
But if you need more time with what's already stirred,
trust that, too.

You may already be practicing graceful resilience
just by being present with what's real.

This chapter isn't about fixing or arriving,
but about staying kind and steady,
even when the pressure rises.

It focuses on the many forms of grace:
practice,
posture,
presence.

Like the Buffalo

When a storm approaches,
most animals run away.

But buffalo walk into the storm,
facing it head-on,
minimizing how long they remain inside it.

They don't resist the discomfort.
They move through it with purpose and instinct.

This is what graceful resilience asks of us:
instead of avoiding life's pain
or holding ourselves to impossible standards,
we must trust that we can move through hard things
without abandoning ourselves.

Resilience doesn't ask for perfection,
only presence.

It's the practice of facing discomfort
with breath,
with softness,
with truth,
with consistent intention,
even when it's hard.
Especially when it's hard.

You don't have to prove your worth through effort.
You simply return to yourself,
again and again,
with compassion.

This is the quiet strength we're learning to trust:
instead of trying to conquer the storms,
we can find steadiness within them.

And sometimes,
embodying that kind of grace
doesn't look brave or poetic;
it looks like barely holding it together,
like breathing through another impossible day.

I know that place.

When Grace Finds You in the Mess

Life doesn't always let up.

Sometimes it presses in,
whether with financial strain,
emotional weight,
or physical exhaustion that leaves us breathless.

I know that space intimately.

There were seasons when I was holding more than felt possible:
balancing single parenthood,
managing bills,
and trying to care for my own body and spirit in the cracks between
responsibilities.

And yet,
it was in those very moments,
when I felt the most frayed,
that I began to uncover something unexpected:

grace.

It wasn't polished or perfect,
the kind that arrives when everything is resolved.

It was the kind that meets you in the mess,
that steadies your breath when your world feels like it's falling apart.

Grace is more than survival.
It's how we meet life's weight without letting it collapse our spirit.

It's the quiet strength that says,
Even now, I am still here.

You, too, can find the strength
to practice grace,
not only after the pressure lifts,
but while you're still inside it.

Early Challenges and New Beginnings

After my separation,
re-entering the workforce felt like stepping into the unknown.

I had been working in some form since I was eight years old,
from odd jobs as a kid
to building a professional counseling career.

When my first daughter was born,
I made the choice to step away from my career
to stay home with her—and later, her sister—full-time.

It was hard work.
And it was the greatest privilege of my life.

For a little over three years,
my days were filled with caring for them:
nurturing them, supporting them, building a home rooted in love.

Then came my separation,
and I found myself needing to work again.

But it was more than a job I needed.
My entire sense of identity
and stability
had to be deconstructed and rebuilt from the ground up.

There was no blueprint,
only trial, error, and trust that somehow,
the path would rise to meet me.

Yet even in the uncertainty,
a quiet dream began to take shape:

I wanted to create a space where I could heal
and help others heal, too.

When my daughters were five and eight,
I walked away from work environments that had become stifling,
so tangled in red tape and regulation
that the joy of being a healer had been stripped away.

I chose to build something that felt meaningful,
something that honored who I was becoming.

I took a leap and opened my private practice.

It was terrifying.

I had no savings,
no safety net.
Only conviction.

Every session was a sacred space,
an invitation to guide others while gently unraveling parts of myself.

Each client became a mirror,
reflecting parts of my own journey.

Over the next sixteen years,
my practice became more than a career.

It became a sanctuary,
a space of purpose, healing, and presence.

And just as importantly,
it gave me the flexibility to be present for my girls.

That mattered more than anything.

Building a life rooted in meaning gave me new strength,
but it didn't erase the pressures that would come.
If anything, it taught me how to meet them differently:
not with force, but with grace.

Motherhood and Grace

I had dreamed of being a mother for as long as I could remember.
And once I became one,
I refused to let someone else raise my daughters.

So I built my life around them,
never perfectly,
but always with deep intention.

I carved out moments that became sacred:
- hikes with one child on my back and the other on my front,
- bedtime snuggles that lingered long after the lights were out,
- shared meals that became rituals of connection and grounding.

I gladly gave everything I had.

Still,
there were days when the pressure felt unbearable.

When every bill felt like a mountain.
When exhaustion made even the smallest task feel impossible.

I used to believe that resilience meant pushing harder,
doing more,
toughing it out.

But grace under pressure reminded me of the true meaning of
resilience:

that sometimes, the strongest thing we can do...
is bend.

Not break.
Not collapse.
Lean in.

I had to trust that even in the mess and fatigue,
I could find a way to hold my center.

Grace wasn't something I earned.
It was something I chose,
over and over,
even in the middle of an uncertain storm.

The Weight of Transition

In the beginning,
the girls' visits with their father were irregular,
woven into the weeks without much structure.

Because we still lived in the same city,
the handoffs were manageable,
at least logistically.

Emotionally,
they were anything but.

Every exchange felt like a fresh wound,
a quiet reminder that life, as we had known it, had shifted for good.

Then we moved,
and everything changed.

When my daughters were one and four,
the occasional visits turned into scheduled trips.

Every other weekend,
I packed them into the car
and drove about two hours one way
to a halfway meeting point.

It was a neutral spot that never actually felt neutral,
a place on the map where I handed them over
and watched them disappear into a world I wasn't part of.

The drive there was all about holding it together.
I kept the energy light with
music, snacks, and reassuring smiles.

Anything to make the transition easier on them.

But the drive back alone?
That's when the weight set in.

Some nights,
I gripped the wheel in exhausted silence.

Other times,
I wept,
tears spilling over as the highway blurred around me.

And on the hardest nights,
I screamed into the emptiness of the car,
releasing what I had swallowed down for days:
the grief,
the rage,
the ache of separation.

Then came Sunday:
same drive,
different weight.

I felt relief as I brought my girls home,
mixed with the ache of knowing we'd do it all again in two weeks.

And still, I reminded myself,
We are building something strong.
We will find our way through this.

Healing While Holding It All

At first,
I filled those travel weekends
(really just Saturdays)
with "have-tos":

cleaning,
catching up on work,
running errands.

Anything to stay busy.
Anything to avoid the silence of my daughters' absence.

I stayed in motion,
thinking that if I could just keep going,
I wouldn't have to feel so much.

But eventually,
I realized something:

Busyness isn't the same as healing.
I would not heal this pain if all I did was run from it.

So, little by little,
I began to reclaim those Saturdays.

I took hikes that led me deep into the woods,
where I could finally exhale.

I returned to yoga,
not so much for fitness
as for release, for grounding.

I let myself be still,
even when it felt unnatural.

I journaled,
without pressure to figure everything out,
simply to hear myself think.

It was awkward at first,
like I was breaking some unspoken rule
that said I always had to be doing something more productive.

But over time,
I began to understand the truth:

Caring for myself wasn't indulgent;
it was essential.

Physical and Emotional Healing

Healing,
I began to realize,
didn't mean easing symptoms.
It was making space
for emotions I had buried for years.

I had already been eating nutrient-dense foods,
moving my body, journaling, practicing yoga—
doing the things I knew could support my well-being and healing.
But something shifted.

I began nourishing myself with heart-centered intention and love.
Food became medicine, not just fuel.
Movement became a way of honoring my body, not fixing it.
I moved with love instead of pressure.
I made space for rest,
for hydration,
for stillness.

I deepened the practices that had always circled the edges of my life,
but this time,
I met them with presence, compassion, and reverence.
Yoga became a ritual of release.
Stillness became a sanctuary.
Hot baths became moments of exhale.
Journaling became a conversation
with the parts of me I had long silenced.

I focused on healing body and mind together,
knowing they couldn't be separated.
I fine-tuned a nutrient-dense, anti-inflammatory diet to support my
recovery.
I prioritized rest and movement in equal measure.
I honored what my body asked for,
whether it was a walk,
a nap,
or a deep, guttural cry.

And yet,
healing wasn't linear.
My body continued to remind me of that.
I faced ongoing immune system challenges,
relentless joint and muscle pain,
the burden of endometriosis,
and the recurring agony of kidney stones.

Some days,
progress felt invisible.
But I kept going.

Because underneath it all, I believed,
Healing is possible.

And despite everything—
the exhaustion,
the uncertainty,
the ache of separation—
I held on to the quiet but unwavering belief
that there was still more ahead:

more healing,
more life,
more love
for me
and for my girls.

Breaking the Cycle

As I healed
physically, emotionally, and spiritually,
I began to see more clearly the patterns I had carried.

Some were my own,
but many were inherited.

And in subtle moments,
I could see how those patterns,
those old survival scripts,
were beginning to ripple out into my daughters,
even as I worked tirelessly to create something different.

There were times their voices weren't fully heard,
times when I missed what they needed
because I was overwhelmed or dysregulated.

Sometimes I reacted from a place of wounding
instead of wisdom.

But the difference between their upbringing and mine
is that when I did these things,
I owned it.

I wasn't afraid to apologize,
sincerely, thoughtfully, without defensiveness.

I wanted them to know the truth:

Conflict is not the end.
Repair matters.
Love includes accountability.
Mistakes happen, because we're human.
But forgiveness is possible.
And healing is always available
when we're willing to show up with honesty and care.

I was determined to give them a different kind of childhood,
one rooted in safety, visibility, and unconditional love.

There would still be struggle,
but also truth and tenderness.

Coming from where I did,
I believe I did a pretty good job.

Through it all,
we stayed connected.
We found our rhythm.
We kept laughing.
We kept loving.

We became the "Can-Do Girls."

We were resilient,
creative,
and capable of facing whatever came our way
with humor, grit, and grace.

The longer visits to their dad's house
during holidays and summers
were layered.

I didn't love the distance.
But I chose to use that time to care for myself.

Even as I tried to forge a new path,
I could feel the old patterns tugging at me:

Fix it.
Be available.
Carry the weight.

Yet even in the tension,
I knew otherwise:

We were growing.
We were healing.
We were becoming.

And I was quietly proud to be where I was:
imperfect,
but anchored in love.

Our life was not rooted
in the past,
but in the possibility of what could be.

Practicing Grace Under Pressure

Grace isn't about pretending the pressure doesn't exist,
nor about pushing through or bypassing what's hard.

It's about moving with the weight of life,
with all parts of yourself aligned.

It's learning how to stay rooted in the storm,
how to soften without collapsing,
how to trust your body, your spirit, and your truth,
even when nothing feels certain.

Here are five foundational ways to embody grace under pressure:

1. Recognize the Small Wins: Your Nervous System Is Always Listening

Physical: Celebrate micro-movements of care, like stretching, drinking water, or eating something nourishing.
Emotional: Acknowledge the moments you chose grace over self-criticism.
Mental: Shift focus from what's unfinished to what you've already moved through.
Spiritual: Trust that even the smallest steps forward are divinely guided.

When you notice what's working,
your nervous system feels it.

You don't have to wait for a breakthrough to celebrate progress.

2. Stay Present, Even in the Chaos

Physical: Use grounding tools, like feeling your feet on the earth, placing a hand on your heart, or breathing into your belly.
Emotional: Let feelings surface. Let them move through instead of numbing or bypassing.
Mental: Anchor into the now. Resist the urge to solve the future.
Spiritual: Remember that presence is faith in motion. It says, *This moment matters.*

You don't have to be consistently calm.
You just have to stay present in what's real.

3. Surrender Is Not Weakness; It's Wisdom

Physical: Pause and ask, *Where am I holding this in my body?* Then release it.
Emotional: Let go of the idea that control equals safety.
Mental: Loosen your grip on needing a solution. Allow life to unfold.
Spiritual: Keep in mind that surrender is a doorway to divine support, a yes to unseen help.

Letting go isn't giving up;
it's creating space for what wants to come through.

4. Renewal Happens in Micro-Moments

Physical: Let out a deep exhale. Spend two minutes in the sun. Stretch between meetings.
Emotional: Notice small moments of peace, comfort, or laughter.
Mental: Protect your energy, limit doom scrolling, and say no to unnecessary pressure.
Spiritual: Remember the sacred is in the ordinary. Let beauty catch you off guard.

You don't need a retreat to begin again.
You only need a moment
and permission to honor it.

5. Lean on Others: Isolation Is Not Strength

Physical: Let someone carry a bag for you, make you tea, or simply sit beside you.
Emotional: Share your heart with someone who sees you clearly.
Mental: Remind yourself, *I don't have to do this alone.*
Spiritual: Support is everywhere; ask for it and be open to how it arrives.

True strength includes connection.
It welcomes help without shame.
It lets love in.

Invitation

Before you begin,
create a space that feels supportive.

Move your body: stretch, sway, shake out what feels stuck.
Let your breath lead you.
Find a spot that grounds you:
your favorite chair, a quiet corner,
or a blanket beneath an open sky.

Gather what you need:
a journal and pen, your laptop,
or even a voice recorder if words come more easily aloud.

Bring a favorite drink,
something soothing, something steadying.
Breathe.
Feel yourself arrive.

This is sacred space,
just for you.

Reflection Prompts

Let these questions be a doorway
into self-trust, self-tending, and grace under pressure.

1. **Recognizing Small Wins**
   - What is one small victory I've had this week, either physically, emotionally, mentally, or spiritually?
   - How can I celebrate or honor myself for it?

2. **Presence and Connection**
   - How often do I allow myself to be fully present with others?
   - What are simple ways I can bring more presence into my relationships?

3. **Surrender and Trust**
   - Where in my life am I resisting what is?
   - What would it look like to surrender, just a little, to what's unfolding?

4. **Micro-Moments of Renewal**
   - What small acts of care bring me back to myself?
   - How can I weave these moments into my day, without guilt?

5. **Receiving Support**
   - Where in my life do I still try to carry it all alone?
   - What's one step I can take to let help, love, or support in?

As you reflect,
let your body guide you.

If a question stirs something, pause.
If an answer feels heavy, breathe into it.
If resistance arises, ask,
What part of me is afraid of this truth?

Let this be a conversation
with your whole self:
body, mind, spirit.

When you're done,
thank yourself for showing up.
This, too, is grace.

Next Steps

Grace under pressure is a practice,
not a performance.

As you move through your days,
consider these invitations:
Celebrate one small win out loud.
Say no to something you don't have capacity for.
Let someone help you—without apology.
Build in a micro-moment of renewal: a breath, a prayer, a warm mug
in your hands.
Speak gently to yourself in a moment you'd normally push harder.

Choose one aligned action.
Let it be enough.

Integration

Grace isn't loud.
It's the breath you remember to take.
The softness in your eyes
when you look at yourself with love.

Let this moment be enough.
Let it steady you.
Let it carry you forward.

CHAPTER 6

The Space I Choose

"You may not control all the events that happen to you,
but you can decide not to be reduced by them."
—Maya Angelou

Where We've Been, Where We're Going

In Chapter 5,
we explored how grace meets us both in stillness and in motion,
how it rises within us even when life presses in.

We learned that grace under pressure doesn't require performance,
only presence.
It's the soft strength that allows us to stay grounded in the chaos,
to breathe through intensity,
and to care for ourselves when the world demands more than we
can give.

Now, we turn inward again:
After finding steadiness in the storm,
we rebuild the foundation beneath us.

We begin to reflect on the messages we've absorbed
about worth, love, and what it means to protect our peace.

This is the heart of healing:
remembering who you are
and learning how to live from that truth.

The Ground Beneath Your Becoming

On the journey of healing and self-discovery,
three essentials form the foundation of lasting transformation:

self-worth, self-love, and boundaries.

These are more than concepts;
they're living practices.

They shape how you move through the world,
how you treat yourself,
and how you allow others to treat you.

They are the ground beneath your becoming.

When you reclaim your worth,
when you learn to love yourself as you are,
and when you hold clear, compassionate boundaries,
you step into a life that reflects your truth.

A Lifetime of Self-Sufficiency

I've always been strong,
always been independent.

It wasn't a brand-new thought,
but one day, the question landed differently:
Why am I still doing this alone?

That question wasn't just about relationships;
it was about how I had lived my entire life.

Growing up in an unsafe home,
I learned early on that no one was coming for me.

Connection was something I craved
but had no healthy model for.

I became self-sufficient because I had to be.

And yet, even in my independence,
I longed for companionship, connection, and community.

The brain gravitates toward what's familiar,
even when it wounds us.

Unless we dig deep, we repeat the patterns we know.
But I'd been digging for a long time,
peeling back layers, naming patterns,
healing what once felt unhealable.
And still, I wondered,
How much further do I have to go?

Even as I began cultivating healthier friendships,
I could feel the old belief still humming underneath:
I have to do it all myself.
It was so deeply wired in me,
so familiar,
that even love sometimes felt like a risk.

What the Mirrors Taught Me

Every relationship is a mirror,
but the ones that stir something deep within us
are the ones that reveal the most.

These are the ones we risk something for,
the ones we open ourselves up to.

A few years after my divorce,
I began dating again, slowly and intentionally.
I hadn't dated much before marriage,
so everything felt unfamiliar,
a terrain I was learning as I went.

My daughters remained my deepest priority,
but I was also open:
to growth,
to love,
to something real.

I brought everything I had been learning with me.
I showed up with sincerity,
with hope,
with care.

And I knew, even as I tried,
I would not settle.

Some mirrors exposed my tendency to overgive,
to try and earn love by being more:
more patient,

more understanding,
more accommodating.

Others revealed my fear of being "too much"
or of asking for anything at all.

Some showed me the ache of being unseen,
even when I was right beside someone.

And the hardest ones
reflected how deeply I still believed
I had to work for love.

Mirrors invite us to see what's hidden.
But they can also invite collaboration and mutual evolution—
if we're willing to see clearly,
and if we choose the right ones.

Not all mirrors are easy to look into.
Some reflect our light.
Some reveal our shadows.
Some distort,
and some clarify.

But all offer insight
if we look with openness and discernment,
if we're willing to choose ourselves in the reflection.

The relationships that meet us in truth
don't just show us who we've been;
they remind us of who we're becoming.

They hold up insight, not illusion.
They help facilitate growth, healing, and even repair,
as long as both people are willing to do the work.

When chosen wisely, mirrors become sacred invitations
to return to our wholeness.

Even the painful ones—
the reflections chosen from old patterns
before I could fully see—
weren't punishments.
They were lessons.
They were redirections.

Some encounters were only a sentence.
Some, a paragraph.
Some were long enough to feel like chapters.

But each one shaped me.

What felt like loss was often protection.
What felt like abandonment was often release.
What seemed like rejection was sometimes misalignment,
a quiet truth rising beneath the ache.

Rejection, I've come to realize,
is divine redirection.

And for that,
I am truly grateful.

I gleaned something meaningful from each mirror.

I learned.
I healed.
I grew.

And where there was kindness, connection, or beauty,
I hold gratitude for that, too.

Because every reflection,
no matter how long it lingered,
offered a piece of the path
that led me here.

Seeing Potential vs. Accepting What Is

For most of my life, I saw people's potential, that is,
their highest, truest self,
even when they couldn't see it in themselves.

I believed in what was possible.
I saw who someone could become.

And while that felt like a gift,
I've since learned that potential, on its own, isn't enough.

Potential must be grounded in reality.
It must be chosen, owned, and acted upon
by them, not just held by me.

Because no matter how much I believed in someone's capacity to
become their true self,
if they weren't willing or ready to choose that path,
I was the one doing all the work.

I was the one exhausting myself.

Hoping someone would become who I knew they could be,
waiting for them to "get it,"
trying to be the catalyst for their transformation—
that wasn't love.
That was self-sacrifice.

Love is not a waiting game.
It's not a project.
And it's certainly not meant to be earned through endurance.

One of the most revealing truths I've come to understand is this:
We can only meet others as deeply as we've met ourselves.

And when I stayed in relationships built on nothing but potential,
I was abandoning myself.

The most loving thing I could do—for them and for myself—
was to accept them exactly as they were,
not for who they could be
or who I hoped they might become.

If who someone is aligns with you, you can walk beside them.
If it doesn't, you can release them with love.

Don't think of it as rejection
or judgment,
but as clarity.

Because love does not mean staying where you are not fully seen.
Connection is not meant to be built by waiting for someone to
become ready.

Let them be where they are.
And let yourself move forward with grace, with truth, and without
apology.

The Truth About Being "Too Much"

For a long time, I believed I was too much:
too intense, too emotional, too honest.

But in truth,
I was real.
I showed up fully.
I loved with intention.

I was present.

And that kind of presence reveals things.
It reveals whether someone can meet you in the depths they claim
they want.
It exposes the gap between what someone says they're ready for
and what they're truly capable of receiving.

My depth was never the problem.
It was the mirror that reflected what others hadn't yet made peace
with in themselves.

My presence asked for accountability
and authenticity.

It asked to be met, not managed.

And for some, that felt like a threat.

Because being seen, truly seen, can be terrifying
when you're still hiding from yourself.

I don't say this with bitterness.
I say it with love, with grace, and with hard-earned clarity.

My love has never been too much.
But it has been too honest for those who weren't ready to be honest
with themselves.

The Mirror That Changed Everything

There was a relationship—brief but intense—
that revealed a pattern I thought I had already healed.

Someone once asked me
if what I had experienced in this dynamic was codependency.
Yes, to some extent,
but it was codependency on steroids.

Traditional codependency often looks like self-sacrifice,
people-pleasing,
and attaching your worth to being needed.
It can be quiet,
chronic,
and normalized.

Trauma bonding takes that even further.
Trauma-bonded codependency is volatile,
addictive,
and intense.
It hijacks your nervous system.

The highs feel euphoric.
The lows feel unbearable.
The person becomes both the drug and the pain.

I've since learned that this kind of relationship
activates the brain's reward system
in the same way heroin or cocaine might.

The moments of closeness,
the intensity,
the longing and relief—
they all light up the dopamine system, creating a high.

Meanwhile, the inconsistency,
the absence,
and the emotional starvation between those highs
creates withdrawal.

And so, we chase the next hit,
because that withdrawal is excruciating.

Breadcrumbing,
laying out those occasional crumbs of affection or attention,
only reinforces the cycle.

We hold on for the next small dose,
hoping it will finally be enough.

The hardest part
is that this wasn't new to me.
I had felt this before
in another relationship.

And before that,
I had learned it from my parents.
From my mom,
who could be warm and loving one moment
and emotionally unavailable the next.

From my dad,
whose love felt distant, conditional, and just out of reach.

From the emotional whiplash of being the one
who soothed,
adjusted,
and overfunctioned
just to stay connected.

That kind of inconsistency becomes familiar.
And what's "familiar,"
the nervous system often mistakes for "safe."

This wasn't love;
it was survival.
And it was insidious.

I knew I had to leave,
but leaving felt impossible.
The relationship was so addictive,
and not in the casual sense of the word:
in the neurological,
body-altering,
trauma-reinforcing sense.

I thought I had healed that part of me.
And in many ways, I had.

I had tended to it
to the extent I understood then.
I had addressed layer after layer,
growing in ways I once thought impossible.

But this experience showed me
there were still places within me that needed witnessing,
parts of me still aching for love,
protection,
and presence.

It took time,
so much time,
to learn that love doesn't have to hurt,
that I don't have to chase closeness
or earn attention
or endure inconsistency to feel seen.

The day I walked away from that relationship,
I was doing more than leaving him;
I was finding myself,
reclaiming my peace,
interrupting the pattern.
I was finally learning to give myself
the love I had always longed for.

I Will Not Abandon Me

He walked ahead of me,
not ten steps,
but just far enough
to make a statement:
to remind me
where he stood.
And where I didn't.

I didn't call it strength,
but I *felt* it:
that subtle absence of reach,
the space that said,
Try harder.
Prove more.

And I did.
I convinced myself
he would eventually see me,
eventually love me.
But he didn't even know
how to love himself.

Still,
I voiced my needs.
I drew my lines.
And I was met
with ridicule dressed as reason,
dismissal served cold
like logic.

He talked nonstop about himself,
center stage every time.
And when he asked about me,
it was performative,
fleeting.
He didn't listen to understand.
And I felt it:
the slow slipping away.
So I stopped speaking.
I went inside,
tucked my truth in quiet corners
where at least I could hear it.

I was so proud
of how I'd grown,
how I'd found my voice
and carved out boundaries
with trembling hands.
But pride turned to ache
when I saw the truth:

What I'd fallen into
was not a mistake;
it was a mirror,
a lesson wrapped in thorns,
another storm.
The earth cracked open beneath me,
and I came completely undone.

But being undone
is not destruction;
it is the shedding
before the becoming.

I have been made anew:
soft, sharp,
tender, unshakable.
And I will not stoop
to be seen.
I will not chase
to be chosen.
I will never again
abandon the woman
who rose from her knees,
gathered her light,
and walked forward
without looking back.

As for him?
I hope he heals.
But I've already set down
the weight of waiting.

I Would Find Them

What I thought
was the end of me
was really
a beginning,
one I didn't yet
have words for.

But I would find them.

I Am the Closure

Most relationships weren't meant to last;
they were meant to awaken.

They mirrored the ache I hadn't yet named,
the parts of me that thought
if I loved harder, waited longer, gave more,
maybe they'd choose me.

But pain has a way of becoming clarity
when you're ready to stop performing for crumbs.

This isn't bitterness;
it's sovereignty.

I'm no longer available for confusion disguised as love
or silence parading as power.

I don't need closure from the ones who never truly saw me.
I am the closure.

And I am the beginning
of something wildly true,
undeniably whole,
and deeply mine.

The Boat I Built, the Truth I Found

Around this time,
I went to an energy healing session.

(This was the kind of session that works with the body's energy
centers—
often called chakras—
gently attuning to where emotion, memory, or stress might be
stored.
It's less about diagnosis,
more about intuitive listening and energetic support.)

The practitioner paused at my root chakra.
She saw something:
a vision.

She saw me
alone on a boat,
wooden,
weathered,
rocking in rough waters.

I was fiercely self-sufficient,
equipped for the storm
and prepared for whatever came next.

I had been navigating rough seas
for as long as I could remember:
fighting off sea serpents,

patching leaks,
steering through the unknown,
and handling it all with precision and skill.

Because that's what I knew how to do.
That's what kept me safe.

And yet,
something in me was quietly asking,
Why am I doing this by myself?

I saw it clearly.
Yes, I knew how to survive.
Yes, I had always found a way through.

But now,
something deeper was declaring,
I don't want to do it alone anymore.

Months later,
in another healing session—this time focused on my throat chakra—
the message came through even clearer,
this time through voice.

It wasn't forced.
It surfaced naturally,
as if it had been waiting for me to speak it:

*"I know I got me...
but I want someone else to 'got me,' too."*

There it was,
the part of me that had always longed for mutual support
but had learned to survive by expecting none.

The truth was no longer avoidable:
I had spent a lifetime proving I didn't need anyone.
But what I truly desired...was to be met.

Not carried.
Not saved.

But seen,
held,
supported.

And I hoped that maybe, just maybe,
I could have the kind of love I didn't need to earn,
the kind of love I could simply receive.

No Longer Earning Love, Simply Receiving It

The realization of wanting a better kind of love
didn't arrive in a single lightning-bolt moment.

It was cumulative:
a quiet unraveling of old stories
and a lifetime of connecting the dots,
of breaking cycles,
of setting myself free.

Because receiving love—without having to earn it—requires
openness.
And for so long, I had kept myself braced,
protected,
guarded, and justifiably so.

I didn't trust love to hold me,
so I held myself tightly against its absence.

But something fundamental began to shift,
mostly over years of healing,
but especially through one connection
that stirred up old wounds in new ways.

Again, I felt the need to fix,
to rescue,
to prove my worth through sacrifice.

But this time,
I began choosing differently,
even when it hurt,
even when it felt impossible.

I see myself now.
I hear myself.
I value myself.
I support myself.

And because of that,
I no longer keep myself hidden.
I no longer protect myself from being fully seen,
heard,
or supported.

I don't need love to save me.
I don't need connection to complete me.

But I am open to receiving it—
with ease instead of effort.

These days, love feels easy,
at least with my daughters
and my closest friends.

And when romantic love comes,
I know there will still be moments of uncertainty.
Old wounds will resurface.

But I am not who I used to be.

I no longer overextend to be chosen.
I no longer shrink to be accepted.
I no longer silence my needs for someone else's comfort.

I move slower now,
with intention,
with love,
with self-respect.

I know who I am.
And I love her.

And when love comes,
I won't chase it.
I will receive it.
I will savor it.

Because I have already found home
within myself.

Returning to the Foundation

To be truly open to love—
the kind we receive without earning—
we must also look at what has stood in the way.

This is where self-worth deepens,
self-love roots itself,
and boundaries begin to take shape.

And it begins by meeting shame
with truth.

The Weight of Shame

Before we can fully reclaim our self-worth,
we have to talk about shame.

Shame is the silent story that says,
There's something wrong with me.

It doesn't say you made a mistake,
but that you *are* a mistake.

It's different from guilt.
Guilt can be a healthy response
when our actions don't align with our values.
It points us toward repair.
Guilt says, *I did something wrong.*

Shame, on the other hand, pulls us into hiding.
It disconnects us from others
and from ourselves.

Shame is one of the oldest survival strategies we carry.
We absorb it early
through rejection, punishment, disconnection, or unmet needs.

It teaches us to shrink,
to please,
to hide,
to perform,
to stay small so we don't get hurt again.

But shame was never truth;
it was protection.

It's how the younger you tried to make sense of chaos.
If you were the problem,
then maybe you could fix it.

That illusion gave you a sense of control
at a time when you had none.

But now?

You don't need shame to keep you safe.
You need truth.
You need love.

You need to remember that your worth was never missing,
only buried.

Releasing shame doesn't mean erasing the past.
You're meeting it with compassion,
naming the stories that were never yours to carry.
And you're choosing to believe something new.

You don't have to know how yet.
We'll get there,
one breath,
one truth,
one small act of self-love at a time.

Already Worthy

Your worth is not something you have to earn,
prove,
or fight for.

It has always been yours.

But many of us were taught otherwise.
We learned to tie our value to what we could produce,
how we performed,
or how well we met the needs of others.

We learned that being "enough" meant doing enough,
giving enough,
pleasing enough.

And over time, we forgot the truth:
We are worthy simply because we exist.

Self-worth doesn't come from being perfect
or achieving some ideal version of yourself.
It comes from remembering who you are
beneath the layers,
the programming,
the expectations,
and the fear.

Reclaiming your worth isn't about becoming someone new.
It's about returning to yourself.

Your past does not define your worth.
Your mistakes do not diminish it.
Your value is not up for negotiation.

This is not something you need to strive for,
but something you are allowed to remember.

Love Starts Here

Self-love is not something you give yourself as a reward once you've earned it.
It is the foundation beneath every aligned relationship,
including the one you have with yourself.

Many of us were taught that love had to be earned
through sacrifice, performance,
or the ability to meet someone else's needs.

Growing up, I often heard the Bible verse
"Love the Lord your God... Love your neighbor..."

But the rest was usually left off:
"...as yourself."

It was spoken in Sunday School,
woven into sermons and spiritual conversations,
but the emphasis was always on others:
Serve more.
Give more.
Be good.
Be selfless.

No one ever talked about the *"as yourself"* part.
And yet, there it was:
an invitation to love others *from* the way we love ourselves,
not instead of.

But I internalized the message another way:
that loving others meant shrinking,
sacrificing,
and staying small.

Several years ago,
I began to question that narrative.
I started gently naming it with friends
and with clients who invited the conversation.

What if the *"as yourself"* part was never meant to be silent?
What if loving yourself is not selfish
but essential
for truly loving others well?

The truth is,
you cannot truly love others beyond the way you love yourself.
To the extent you meet yourself with compassion, tenderness, and care,
you are able to extend that same depth to others.

We learned how to pour love outward,
but not how to receive it inward.
We learned to abandon ourselves in the name of connection.

But real self-love is not selfish
or indulgent.
It is essential.

Self-love is the practice of standing in your own corner,
of treating yourself with the same kindness, presence, and care
that you so freely offer others.

For me, it's how I rise in the morning:
not leaping into urgency,
but waking gently, stretching slowly,
and easing into the day with grace.

It's how I listen to my body's cues.
Hunger? I nourish myself.
Thirst? I hydrate.
Restlessness or pain?
I walk, stretch, or soak in a bath filled with Dead Sea salt.

It's putting down my phone
to take in the sunlight on the leaves,
the shape of a cloud,
or the way a bird sings just outside the window.

These small acts feed my nervous system.
They anchor me in beauty.
They remind me I am worth this kind of care,
this kind of noticing,
this kind of love.

Self-love means turning toward every part of you.
You don't have to push them away
or shame them into silence;
you can welcome them home.

Like the part of me that still wants to say yes,
to show up, to support, to give,
even when I'm running on empty.

Now, I choose myself.
I honor my capacity,
even when someone else expects more,
even when saying no feels tender.

That is self-love, too:
refusing to abandon myself to be chosen,
refusing to silence my needs to be safe.

To love yourself is to hold yourself.
To hold yourself is to know yourself.
And to know yourself is to trust yourself.

And here's the truth:
The parts of you that feel most unlovable or undesirable
are often the ones that need your love the most.

They don't need more judgment.
They need your gentleness,
your presence,
your acceptance,
your unconditional care.

Not after they've healed
or been "fixed,"
but now,
as they are.

Self-love isn't just a feeling;
it's a commitment,
a practice,
a daily choice.

Some days, it won't feel easy.
Some days, just getting out of bed,
eating a nourishing meal,
or taking a deep breath is a victory.

And that's okay.

Trying counts.
Effort, especially if imperfect, is a form of self-love.

Whether it's drinking water,
stepping outside,
or speaking to ourselves kindly,
these small acts build trust.

They teach our nervous system that we are safe in our own care,
that we can depend on ourselves.

And here's the powerful part:
Repetition and consistency don't just create new habits;
they create new neural pathways.

Each time we show love to ourselves, even in small ways,
we're rewiring our brains for safety, worthiness, and self-trust.

We're no longer just thinking differently;
we're becoming different.

And over time, this becomes a foundation of love
we no longer have to reach for,
because it lives within us.

And sometimes, it looks like discipline.
Discipline is self-love in action.
It's how we show up for ourselves when no one else is watching.

It's choosing to nourish our body,
honor our energy,
and protect our peace,
over and over again.

If self-love feels unfamiliar, begin here:

Self-awareness:
Who are you outside of what you do for others?
What lights you up?

Self-compassion:
Can you give yourself grace to be in process,
to grow at your own pace?

Self-celebration:
Do you acknowledge your own growth?
(Even the smallest step counts.)

Self-discipline:
Are you keeping the promises you make to yourself?
Or do you abandon your own needs when no one's holding you
accountable?

When you truly learn to hold yourself,
you no longer need to search outside of you
for love to feel whole.

If your answers feel tender, incomplete, or hard to face,
that's okay.

Awareness is where transformation begins.
You're not here to fix everything all at once.
You're here to meet yourself honestly
and begin again,
with gentleness,
with choice,
with presence.

Every honest answer is an invitation.
Every moment of awareness is a doorway.
Start there.

The Sacred Line

Setting boundaries can feel uncomfortable,
especially if we were taught that saying no
means being selfish, difficult, or unlovable.

But here's the truth:
Without boundaries,
we absorb the energy, emotions, and expectations of others,
often at the expense of our own well-being.

We overfunction,
overgive,
overstretch.

We lose ourselves in the roles we play
and forget who we are.

Without boundaries,
love turns into sacrifice,
resentment,
or silent suffering.

But with boundaries,
love becomes a space of mutual respect,
emotional safety,
and freedom.

Boundaries don't push love away;
they make space for real love to exist.

Boundaries are not walls
or ultimatums.
They are not selfish.

Boundaries are self-respect in action.

And we can't just set them with others;
we must also set them with ourselves.
They're how we honor our own energy,
our own needs,
our own limits.

Boundaries protect not just you
but the integrity of your connections.

Setting a boundary doesn't mean controlling others.
You're simply preserving clarity for yourself.

Here are some guiding principles for setting boundaries:

Know your limits:
What are you no longer available for?
Maybe it's saying yes to every late-night text
or tolerating criticism disguised as closeness.
Maybe it's carrying someone else's emotional weight
long after your arms have gone numb.

Let no be enough:
No is a complete sentence.
You don't have to explain your peace.
Saying, "I'm not available this weekend,"

without guilt or justification, is enough.
Silence after your no is not a void to fill;
it's a space to honor.

Protect your energy:
If something drains you,
it's your responsibility to step back, not to endure.
Maybe it's declining a call when your body asks for rest,
or maybe it's choosing not to re-engage in a conversation
that leaves you anxious for days.

When you set a boundary,
you're telling your younger self,
I see you. I hear you. You are safe.

When you hold that boundary,
you teach yourself—maybe for the first time—
I am worthy of protection.

Hold Your Keys

Think of your life as a car
and your keys as your power.

When you give someone your keys,
you're no longer in control of where you're going.
They get to drive.
They choose the route,
the speed,
the music,
the temperature,
the destination.

You might be in the passenger seat
or in the back.
Maybe they've left you in the trunk
or strapped you to the roof.

You're no longer deciding how fast you're going
or how safe you feel.

Boundaries are how we choose the pace of our life.
They're how we regulate the noise,
balance our nervous system,
and protect what matters most inside.

Holding your keys means honoring your capacity.
It means knowing you have a say
in what moves you forward—
and what doesn't get to steer anymore.

And often,
we don't even realize we've handed over our keys
until we're exhausted,
anxious,
or breaking down on the side of the road.

But right now,
you hold the keys.
And you're going to drive.

You decide who gets to ride along
and in what capacity.

You choose which people you'll allow inside the car—
whose opinions, energy, and influence you let in—
and which ones you'll leave at the curb.

If someone is meant to journey with you,
they'll respect your pace,
your preferences,
and your presence.

And if you choose to hand someone the wheel for a while
because you're tired or need support,
that's okay.

The difference is this:
You still hold the keys.

You can take the wheel back at any time.

Don't give away your direction,
your voice,
or your choice.

Hold your keys.

My Boundaries

My boundaries have been hard-earned,
forged in the fires of struggle.
Blood, sweat, and tears brought me here.

Each line I draw is a scar turned sacred,
a testament to the battles I've faced
to reclaim the space I stand in now.

They are not barriers but choices,
crafted from the depths of my journey,
quiet reminders that I am whole.

I am here, unyielding and soft,
strong enough to honor myself
and brave enough to love fully,
because I've fought to love me first.

Living from the Inside Out

When we claim our worth,
practice self-love,
and hold firm to our boundaries,
we begin to live from the inside out.

We no longer chase peace;
we become it.

We no longer seek permission to take up space;
we embody it.

Integrating Self-Worth, Self-Love, and Boundaries

These are not separate practices.
They are interwoven, inseparable, and essential to living in
alignment.

When you reclaim your worth,
self-love naturally follows.

When you truly love yourself,
boundaries become intuitive.

And when you hold your boundaries,
you reinforce your worth.

It becomes a cycle of empowerment,
a shift from striving to honoring,
from proving to remembering,
from performance to presence.

Resistance is normal, of course.
Growth is rarely linear.

But every time you choose to listen inward,
show up for yourself,
or say no with love,
you're rewriting your story in real time.

You're building new neural pathways.
You're becoming the version of you
who no longer abandons herself.

And as this foundation strengthens,
something else begins to rise:

authenticity.

Authenticity cannot be curated.
It's not performance dressed up as truth.

It's the quiet clarity of living as you are,
without needing to explain, prove, or perform.

Self-worth makes authenticity possible.
And authenticity makes freedom inevitable.

More than learning how to care for yourself,
you're learning how to live as your truest self.

And that changes everything.

Moving Forward with Intention

As you reflect, remember this:

You are not who you were when this chapter began.
And you don't need to rush to become someone else.

You are already becoming.
You are already home within yourself.

With every insight, every pause, every conscious choice,
you are shaping a life rooted in wholeness.

You now know how to listen inward,
how to name your needs,
how to protect your peace,
how to choose yourself,
not out of isolation, but out of love.

Let that knowing guide you forward.

There will still be moments of uncertainty.
Old patterns may resurface.

But you are no longer the version of you who abandons herself
to belong.

You know your worth.
You honor your boundaries.
You love yourself in ways that once felt impossible.

And as you move forward,
toward aligned love, nourishing relationships, meaningful work, and
all that is waiting for you,
remember this:

You are no longer waiting.
You are receiving.

You are already whole.
You are already home.

Invitation

Before you begin,
take a moment to check in.

Do you need water? A snack? A walk around the block?
Tend to yourself first.
Then, return here when you're ready.

Find a quiet place where you feel grounded and safe.
Light a candle, wrap yourself in a blanket, or sit beneath an open sky.
Bring your journal, your voice recorder, or just an open heart.

Breathe.
Feel your feet on the ground.
Let your shoulders soften.

This is your space.
This is your time.
Let it meet you exactly where you are.

Reflection Prompts

Let these questions guide you into deeper self-trust
and connection with the truth of who you are becoming.

Reconnect with the parts of you that still need to be seen.
- What did your five-, ten-, and fifteen-year-old selves long for?
- What do they need from you now?

What does self-worth mean to you right now?
- Where do you feel most connected to it?
- Where do you still question it?

How are you practicing self-love?
- Where are you extending compassion?
- Where might you be withholding it?

What old beliefs still shape how you see your worth or lovability?
- What would it look like to release those stories?

Are there parts of you that you still feel ashamed of?
- Where did that shame originate?
- Whose voice might still be lingering?

Where are boundaries needed right now?
- Where are you overextending or overexplaining?
- Where are you longing to say yes—to yourself?

Imagine living fully aligned with your true self.
- What does that version of you look and feel like?
- What's one small step you can take to move toward that today?

When boundary setting feels hard, whose voice do you hear?
- How can you begin to replace that voice with one rooted in truth and compassion?

Next Steps

Here's a visualization to support your ongoing healing:

Healing Through Boundaries

Close your eyes.
Picture your younger self—child or teen—standing before you.
They're holding something:
a belief that used to keep you safe, like
"Saying no means rejection,"
or
"Love must be earned."

Step toward them—not to fix, only to affirm.
Place a hand on their shoulder. Speak gently:

You are safe now.
Your needs matter.
You are allowed to have limits.
You do not have to abandon yourself to be loved.

Let them feel seen.
Let them feel chosen.
Let them know that each time you set a boundary,
you're protecting them, too.

Then breathe.
And carry this truth forward:
Boundaries aren't walls;
they are doors back to yourself.

The Aligned Opportunities I Welcome

With deeper self-worth, self-love, and boundaries,
this is the energy I'm aligned with now.

After more than two decades of deep healing,
raising my daughters with unwavering love,
and fully stepping into myself,
I've gained a clearer sense of the love, connection,
and experiences I'm ready to receive.

But clarity isn't the same as certainty.
And I know my journey is far from complete.

I desire a connection that is both grounded and expansive,
a love that feels like home
but also invites me to stretch,
evolve,
and meet new parts of myself.

I don't need someone to complete me,
and I won't settle for a love that asks me to shrink.

I long for a partner who meets me in the lightness and the depth,
who understands that love doesn't demand perfection,
only asks for showing up,
learning,
and choosing each other with consistency.

But love is not the only thing I'm calling in.
I'm also open to all aligned opportunities:
experiences, collaborations, and connections
that resonate with who I am now.

Not who I used to be,
or who others expect me to be,
but the woman I've become—
and the woman I'm still becoming.

I move with intention,
but I remain open,
knowing life has a way of surprising me
in ways I could never predict.

I no longer seek anything that asks me to dim my light
or abandon my truth to belong.

But I also know
the most meaningful things in life rarely arrive in perfect packages.
They come as invitations
to expand,
to soften,
to surrender into something greater than I could have imagined.

The love I welcome—
whether through relationships, creative work, or soul-aligned
opportunities—
will reflect the self-worth I've cultivated.

But it must also challenge me
in beautiful, life-giving ways.

I'm not chasing.
I'm not striving.
I'm simply ready to receive.

And until then,
I continue to thrive in my own company,
not as someone who has "arrived,"
but as someone who is always unfolding.

I trust that the love, the connections,
and the opportunities meant for me
are already on their way.

And I welcome them
with openness,
with confidence,
and with reverence for the mystery still unfolding.

Pause and notice:
What are you ready to receive
from the wholeness of who you are now?

Integration

Take a breath.
Let your shoulders drop.
Let your heart rest into what you now remember:

You are worthy.
You are lovable.
You are allowed to protect your peace.

You don't need to earn love.
You don't have to prove your worth.
You no longer have to abandon yourself to feel safe.

You belong to yourself now.
Let that be enough for today.
Let that be everything.

CHAPTER 7

Rewriting the Code

"Until you make the unconscious conscious,
it will rule your life and you will call it fate.
I am not what happened to me, I am what I choose to become.
You are what you do, not what you say you'll do."
—Carl Jung

Where We've Been, Where We're Going

In Chapter 6, you explored the foundations of self-worth,

self-love, and the life-giving power of boundaries.
You began choosing yourself in small, daily ways—
and maybe for the first time,
you experienced what it feels like to truly belong to yourself.

But something often happens when we begin honoring our truth:
We uncover what still lives beneath it.

We find old beliefs,
subconscious patterns,
and inherited programming
from childhood, culture, trauma, and survival.

These codes still shape how we see ourselves and the world.
They whisper things like
I'm not allowed to have needs,
I must stay small to be safe, and
I am only lovable if I perform or please.

The difference now is that
we don't just observe
or remember these patterns.

We *reprogram.*
We *rewrite.*

This chapter goes beyond understanding where the story came from
into choosing a new one,
one that reflects who you truly are.

We've explored.
We've uncovered.
Now, we rewrite the code.

Space Between

In the quiet space between endings and beginnings,
I ask, *How many times must I be born again?*

Each time I let go, I descend deeper,
unraveling the layers of what once was,
embracing the gentle emergence of self.

Like a phoenix rising from the ashes
and a lotus blooming from the mud,
I return to forgotten and never-known parts
found only in the shadows of loss.

In surrender, I discover.
In yielding, I find rhythm.

A soft exhale.
A sacred pause.
A rest in the cycle.

I trust in the grace of transformation
as the Divine makes my path known,
as I blossom,
not into someone new,
but into who I've always been.

Honor Your Essence

Learning to honor your essence is a powerful beginning.
But healing doesn't stop at awareness.

We can know we're worthy...
and still feel unworthy.
We can speak about self-love...
and still struggle to receive it.
We can set boundaries...
and still abandon ourselves in the quiet.

That's the nature of old programming:
Even when it no longer serves us, it still feels familiar.
And what's familiar often feels safer than the unknown.

Our nervous system is wired for repetition.
We unconsciously return to roles and beliefs we learned long ago:
to be small,
to be silent,
to overfunction,
to perform for love.

But awareness opens the door.
And intention helps us walk through it.

Once we're inside,
reprogramming is how we begin to shape the space,
how we build a life that reflects our truth
and replace the echoes of the past with something rooted in
the present.

Rewriting the code isn't the same as rewriting the past.
It means choosing again,
replacing old patterns with something truer
that honors who you really are.

This chapter is about that choice,
the uncomfortable, beautiful work
of not only untangling what was never yours,
but retraining your mind, body, and energy
to reflect what always has been:
your freedom,
your power,
your authenticity.

You don't have to keep repeating what was passed down.
You're allowed to interrupt the pattern.
You're allowed to create something new.

Inherited Blueprint and Early Messages

In the very beginning, I was born into
an unstable home that would train me to be small, quiet, and
accommodating,
all out of emotional necessity.

From birth to around age six,
and most significantly up to age two or three,
our neural circuits are wide open.

This is when the foundation of our nervous system is laid.

We don't just learn how to walk and talk;
we learn how safe the world feels.

We learn whether our needs are welcomed or dismissed,
whether our presence brings joy or disruption.

These early blueprints do more than shape our minds;
they live in our cells,
our posture,
our breath,
our choices.

Our mothers shape our inner world from the very beginning,
not only through genetics and mitochondrial DNA,
but through their nervous system, their stress levels, their voice,
their rhythm.

Our fathers contribute equally to our energetic architecture
through presence or absence,
through protection or threat,
through emotional modeling and unspoken rules.

Together, they pass on both gifts and wounds.

And it's in those early moments, before we have words,
that we begin forming beliefs about love, safety, vulnerability, and
worth.

These patterns get etched deep.
But they're not permanent.

They are code,
and code can be rewritten.

Childhood Reflections on Caring Roles

I remember being a small child (under five)
in Central Florida,
aware of things no child should have to carry.

My mom was often in bed,
tired, medicated,
lost in waves of anxiety and depression.

She was addicted to Valium.
And even then,
I felt the quiet panic of her unavailability.

She always said she was tired.
I would later learn
that "tired" often meant something else:
depressed, dysregulated,
shut down by more than exhaustion.

I didn't have words for what I felt,
but my body knew.
And I began to adapt.

I picked tiny berries from the bush outside
and brought them to her,
hoping they might make her feel better.

Even at that age,
I was trying to fix something I didn't cause,
trying to soothe what was never mine to hold.

That was the beginning of my caregiving.

What started as empathy
became identity.

She taught me to accept breadcrumbs,
to silence my own needs,
to place her comfort above my well-being.

And I did,
because even though I did matter,
I had learned
it was safer not to.

Nervous System Regulation
and Letting Go of Roles

Those early experiences shaped me on every level:
developmentally, emotionally, spiritually, energetically.

The fear that my mother might die or leave me alone with my father
became a silent, constant hum in the background of my life.

What had started as anxiety
became a survival tactic.

Even well into adulthood, I could feel it:
that bracing, that hypervigilance,
that deep,
unconscious belief that I existed to care for others,
no matter the cost to myself.

And yet...

through years of nervous system work,
spiritual mentorship, and self-reclamation,
I began to loosen my grip on those roles.

It wasn't instant.
It wasn't clean or linear.

But with every new layer of safety I created in my body,
with every moment I chose presence over performance,
I started to feel something different:
wholeness.

Rewiring the nervous system isn't a formula;
it's a relationship.

It's personal. It's layered. It's sacred.

And for me, it has meant learning to care for myself
as fiercely as I once cared for everyone else.

I was not neglecting others;
I was choosing reverence for my own nervous system
and for the next generation watching me heal.

The Awakening:
"I Am Enough" as a Launch Pad

Like much of my healing,
the process of reprogramming wasn't linear.
It didn't arrive in neat stages or perfect timing.
It came in waves:
through trial and error,
expansion and contraction,
insight and forgetting.

In my mid-to-late twenties and early thirties,
I began to sense that something within me was ready to shift.
I didn't yet have the language
for trauma responses or nervous system regulation.
But I could feel the tension
between who I had been and who I was becoming.

Somewhere along that path,
I encountered a phrase so simple,
it almost felt insignificant:

"I am enough."

At first, it didn't land.
It felt aspirational,
like something meant for other people.
But still, I held on to it.
I whispered it.
I repeated it.
I tested it in moments of doubt.

And slowly,
it began to soften the sharp edges within me.

It didn't feel like a grand revelation.
It felt more like a small key—
one that would eventually unlock everything.

It was during this season
that I joined Dr. Nicole LePera's SelfHealers Circle
in its early days.

That community—
intimate and rooted in intention—
became a sacred turning point.

It reminded me I wasn't alone,
that healing is possible
when we feel seen, supported, and safe.

(Learn more at www.selfhealerscircle.com.)

It gave me tools and language
I didn't even know I was missing.
It reminded me I wasn't broken.

It helped me shift
from analyzing my pain
to actually tending to it,
to feeling it in my body
instead of just naming it in my mind.

I had spent so long
trying to understand my wounds
that I forgot they needed warmth,
not just words.

With gentle curiosity,
I began to reframe my pain
from a problem to solve
to a signal,
a call for safety, presence, and care.

This shift was subtle
but powerful.

As I began to regulate my nervous system
and create more internal safety,
I could finally start to rewrite the code
I'd lived by for decades.

I didn't have to force it.
I achieved this through compassion,
through consistent moments of choosing:
love over fear,
curiosity over judgment,
self-connection over old survival patterns.

That experience catapulted
my self-love, growth, and healing
in ways I'll always be grateful for.

"I am enough"
became more than a mantra.
It became a threshold,
a quiet doorway back to myself.

From that doorway,
I began to see the deeper codes
that had been running the show:

I have to prove my worth.
I need to be everything for everyone.
If I rest, I'm failing.
If I'm not perfect, I'm not lovable.

These were more than passing thoughts.
They were embedded patterns,
protective stories,
inherited survival strategies
dressed up as truth.

"I am enough" was never the finish line;
it was the starting point.

It was the soft landing from which I could begin the real work:
rewriting the code
that no longer matched
who I was becoming.

The Holy Undoing

One of the most painful layers of my healing
was spiritual.

When God is introduced to you
by way of fear, shame, and control,
it can take years
to separate truth from trauma—
if ever.

Many never find their way back.
Some spend their entire lives
feeling cut off from the Divine,
wondering if trust can ever be repaired.

I understood that ache...
but I never lost my connection completely.

Even in my questioning,
even as I sifted through what I'd been taught,
something steady remained within me.

I grew up in a home
where faith was rigid, performative, and punishing.
Christianity was used as a weapon
to enforce silence, obedience, and submission.

The same people who recited Scripture
also harmed children
and protected each other in doing so.

What happens when the very people
who are supposed to represent love...don't?

When God is used to justify harm,
it creates a spiritual wound
that can sever your trust in the Divine—
and in yourself.

I spent years wrestling with that tension.
Part of me longed for connection with God.
Another part was still bracing for punishment.

My spiritual path became a process of unlearning,
pulling apart inherited distortions
from the clarity I felt deep within.

I had to learn how to trust
my own understanding of the Divine:
loving, expansive, relational, and alive.

Healing required that I separate God
from the people who claimed to represent Him—
or anything spiritual or holy.

Thankfully, even as a child,
I sensed something different.

What I felt and experienced of God,
Jesus, the Holy Spirit, and angels
was uniquely my own.

It didn't match what others preached or enforced.
And though I couldn't explain it,
I held on to it.

That quiet knowing stayed with me,
even when I didn't have language for it.

Still, this was one of the most destabilizing
and foundational pieces of my healing.

Without the deconstruction and rebuilding,
without returning to the essence
of all that is holy—
not what people made of it,
but what I knew in my bones—
I wouldn't have found my way back.

And for that,
I am eternally grateful.

Through all the distortion,
a steady presence remained beneath the ache.

I never truly lost my sense
that something sacred was still with me,
protecting and guiding me,
even when I couldn't explain why.

It was jarring to live in that contradiction:
the hypervigilance,
the holding of my breath,
the belief that I had to perform or earn my way to love.

But the purest, most authentic part of me knew this truth:
Nothing was required of me to earn God's love.

I fought fiercely to hold on to that foundation.
And while those lifelines frayed at times,
I never let go.

I was never forsaken.
I was never truly alone.

Over the years, people have asked me
how I still have faith,
how I still trust anything at all.

Sometimes, I haven't had a neat answer.
But deep down, I've always known this:
Something greater was holding me.

Even when I couldn't hold myself.
Even when everything around me seemed to fracture.

Like every other layer of programming,
this one had to be rewritten, too.

Because I couldn't fully reclaim my worth
while still believing
that my very essence needed to be redeemed through suffering.

To begin that rewriting,
I had to go back to the source.

Understanding My Parents' Woundedness

For a long time,
I believed my parents' behavior said something about me.

I believed I wasn't enough,
that I had to try harder,
be better,
do more.

But part of my healing
has been the slow, sometimes painful realization
that they were wounded, too.

My parents didn't wake up one day
and decide to harm or neglect.

They were doing the best they could,
and I don't mean in the idealized way we sometimes use
to dismiss harm,
but truly, with the limited awareness,
tools,
and capacity they had at the time.

That was the best they could do.

Understanding that doesn't excuse everything.
But it does offer perspective.

Their pain was passed down,
like so many unspoken family legacies.

Their coping strategies—
withdrawal, rage, perfectionism, denial—
were survival responses
born of their own unmet needs.

Recognizing this,
while it didn't erase the impact their actions had on me,
did help me stop
personalizing their dysfunction.

It was never about my worth.
It was about their pain.

That shift was essential.

Because until I could see their limitations clearly,
I kept unconsciously trying to earn their love
or repair what was never mine to fix.

Parents give us what they can.

Sometimes it's beautiful.
Sometimes it's barely enough.
Sometimes it hurts.

But I now know
their failures were not reflections of my value.
They were echoes
of their own unhealed stories.

Reflections Through Her Eyes

One afternoon,
my nine-month-old daughter and I were sitting on the kitchen floor.

Sunlight streamed through wide, beautiful windows,
filling the room with warmth.

It was quiet, just the two of us
moving slowly,
playing,
laughing.

Then I noticed her tapping her little finger on the floor.

Something in her expression caught my attention:
not focus,
but distress.

A quiet, rising panic
that no nine-month-old should feel.

She was picking up crumbs,
one by one.

She'd never been told to do that.
She had only seen me do it.

And just like that,
I saw it.

That small act—
something so ordinary, so easy to overlook—
revealed a deeper pattern.

I had always been praised for my cleanliness.
People used to joke
that you could do surgery on my kitchen floor.

I didn't mind the comment,
but in that moment,
the habit landed differently.

Because my spotless kitchen wasn't born of a desire for order;
it came from a need for control.

Clean floors were a survival strategy,
a way to create predictability
in a childhood marked by chaos.

When everything around me felt unstable—
moods, moments,
what might explode or collapse next—
cleaning gave me a sense of control.

If I could keep the floor spotless,
maybe I could stay ahead of the next eruption.
Maybe I could avoid the yelling.
Maybe I could prove I wasn't the problem.

It made me feel useful—
safe, even.

Like I had power
in a house where I often had none.

I had never questioned it,
until I saw it reflected back to me:

in my daughter's tiny hands,
in her quiet mimicry,
in her innocent attempt to follow my lead.

But this was more than imitation.
There was something in her eyes:
a flicker of urgency,
a look of anxiety
that didn't belong on a baby's face.

And that's when it hit me.

She wasn't just copying my behavior.
She was absorbing my energy.

The pressure.
The tension.
The belief that something bad might happen
if things weren't clean enough.

I had made her afraid of something
that didn't even exist for her yet.

And in that mirror,
I finally saw myself:

the way my jaw tightens,
my shoulders rise,
and my chest locks
when I'm trying to scrub away the chaos inside.

Cleaning was never just about tidiness.
It was how I managed the fear,
how I tried to keep everything from falling apart.

That's when the grief rose,
not just for what I had learned,
but for what I had passed down
without realizing.

And still, there was hope.

That moment didn't spiral me into guilt;
it opened a door.

Because if my daughter could mirror my survival strategies,
she could also mirror my growth.

And that's what I began to choose:
to model care instead of control,
presence instead of perfection.

I started leaving the dishes in the sink sometimes.
I let the crumbs stay a little longer.
I sat on the floor with her,
even when there were ten other things I could've cleaned.

I stopped rushing to tidy up before guests arrived.
I let her play freely without hovering.

And when I felt the urge to control the space,
I paused...
and chose connection instead.

I didn't get it right every time,
but it was enough to begin rewiring the pattern.

Now she could see
that safety didn't have to be spotless,
that love could be soft and real,
even in the mess.

I used to believe a parent's window of influence closed at eighteen.
Now I know
it's never too late to change.

Because every step I take toward wholeness—
toward softness, truth, and self-compassion—
becomes a new blueprint
my daughters can carry.

The work of becoming whole
doesn't only heal me;
it sets them free, too.

The Higher Self Speaks

One of the most pivotal shifts in my healing
came through a six-month mentorship
with Devon from Enlighten & Empower,
an intuitive guide and energy healer
who helped me reconnect with a deeper part of myself
I had long forgotten.

During one of our sessions,
Devon shared something she had received intuitively.
It was nothing I had said,
but something she gleaned from a deeper listening.

She explained that she was tuning in to the energy of my Higher Self,
the wiser, whole part of me
that exists beyond conditioning and fear.

What she shared wasn't her opinion
or a suggestion.
It was a message—a soul-knowing—
that she sensed I was ready to hear.

The question wasn't from her to me,
but from me to myself,
from the part of me that had always known the truth:

"Can you accept that the perception you had of yourself was wrong,
not representative of your true essence—
and can you allow that old perspective to die
so that a new perception of self can be born?"

That moment stilled me.
It rippled through every part of my being.

I knew exactly what she meant.

I had been living through a lens shaped by survival,
by trauma, expectation, and old programming.

But that voice within me,
my Higher Self,
was asking me to surrender it.

It wanted me to let go of who I thought I had to be,
to reclaim the truth of who I actually am.

And as I surrendered,
the rewrites expanded,
building on the foundation I had already begun:

I am behind. → *I am right on time.*

Life has to be hard. → *I welcome a life of flow and ease.*

I am alone. → *I am supported—by God, nature, people, and aligned circumstances.*

I must stay small to be safe. → *I am a storm of love. I mirror truth. I take up sacred space.*

I have to give more than I receive. → *I am finding balance in giving and receiving.*

I'm not good at expressing myself. → *I am brilliant. I express authentically, with clarity and confidence.*

These were not mere positive thoughts.
They were codes,
truths I was finally ready to embody.

It's one thing to believe you are worthy in theory.
It's another to let that belief
restructure your nervous system,
rewrite your story,
and rewire you from the inside out.

That was the beginning of a new version of me.

It wasn't someone I was becoming,
but someone I had always been,
now remembered.

The Neuroscience of Change

One of the most empowering discoveries in my healing journey has been this:
Change is always possible,
emotionally and spiritually,
but also biologically and energetically.

Neuroplasticity is the brain's built-in ability to adapt and evolve,
to form new connections, prune outdated ones,
and rewire itself in response to experience.

This means you are not hardwired for suffering or survival mode.
You are wired for *change*.

Neuroplasticity explains why therapy works:
Affirmations, meditation, journaling, breathwork,
new choices, and new thoughts can *actually change your life.*

And the beauty of it
is that it's available to all of us.

No matter your age, your background, or how long a pattern has been in place,
you are never too far gone.
You're never stuck.

Thanks to this remarkable capacity,
both your brain and your heart can rewire themselves
throughout your entire life.

Yes, your heart, too.

The heart doesn't just pump blood;
it has its own intrinsic nervous system,
a wide web of neurons that can sense, respond, and adapt.

It communicates continuously with the brain,
responding to our emotional patterns and experiences.

As researchers describe it:
*"This 'heart brain' is composed of approximately 40,000 neurons
that are alike neurons in the brain, meaning that the heart
has its own nervous system."*[4]

And while it may not store memories like the brain,
its neural circuits do shift and reorganize based on what we feel and
how we live.
In other words, your heart learns how to respond—and it can learn
to respond differently.

In fact, researchers have shown that the heart's nervous system is
highly connected and adaptable, capable of learning and helping
regulate each heartbeat in response to emotional, physical, and
environmental stimuli.[5]

When we begin to heal and shift how we respond emotionally,

---

4 A. M. Alshami, "Pain: Is It All in the Brain or the Heart?," *Current Pain and Headache Reports* 23, no. 88 (2019), https://doi.org/10.1007/s11916-019-0827-4.

5 Giuseppe Giannino et al., "The Intrinsic Cardiac Nervous System: From Pathophysiology to Therapeutic Implications," *Biology* 13, no. 2 (2024): 105, https://doi.org/10.3390/biology13020105.

the heart starts to respond differently, too.
Your brain and heart are in constant communication.
When one begins to shift, the other follows.

Every time you repeat a thought or behavior, you reinforce a pathway—
mostly in your brain,
but perhaps, over time, in your heart's responses, too.

Like a trail in the woods,
it's carved deeper each time you walk it.

The good news is that
you can choose to walk a new path.
And with time, that path will become your new default.

All it takes is practice.
Even the smallest consistent actions send a powerful signal:
This is the new way.

Pause before reacting.
Take a deep breath instead of collapsing into fear.
Notice when an old belief is speaking...and choose not to follow it.

Repeat (with feeling and conviction) a truth like
"I am safe," or "I am worthy,"
until your body begins to believe it.
These are more than affirmations;
they're rewiring tools.

And each time you use them,
you remind your brain and your heart
that change is possible...and safe.

Because healing isn't a single decision.
It's a continuous rewiring,
one moment,
one breath,
one act of self-love at a time.

The Power of Patience and Self-Compassion

Rewiring the brain and heart is possible,
but patience is essential.

Growth doesn't happen all at once;
it happens in layers,
in waves,
in seasons.

Sometimes you'll take five steps forward.
Other times you'll trip over an old belief
and wonder if anything's changed at all.

That doesn't mean you've failed.
It means you're human.
It means you're healing.

Your journey will move like the ocean:
in rhythms, in tides.
There will be moments of acceleration
and moments of stillness.
Neither is a problem.
Both are part of the process.

Just as the nervous system reorganizes itself through repetition
and rest,
your healing requires both movement and pause.

You only need to keep going
without being too hard on yourself.
Notice when you're slipping into old stories
and gently invite yourself forward again.

Respond to your discomfort not with shame,
but with softness.
Ask,
"What do I need right now?"
instead of
"What's wrong with me for feeling this way?"

Because healing isn't just about what you practice;
it's about how you practice:

with compassion,
with grace,
with patience for the parts of you still learning
how to feel safe in a new way of being.

Your body may feel tired after a big shift,
but that doesn't mean you're weak.
Growth takes energy
and integration takes time.

Let that be okay.
The invitation is to trust the pace of your own becoming.

Honor the days that feel fast
and the ones that move like honey.

Listen for the quiet truths
that only rise when you're willing to slow down.

You are not behind.
You are not broken.
You are not doing it wrong.

You're just in a season.
And seasons always shift.

Shifting Your Perspective on Challenges

Challenges are inevitable.
But how you meet them—how you *see* them—can change
everything.

When you're deep in discomfort, it's easy to believe something's
gone wrong.
You're inclined to try to fix it,
to escape it,
or to judge yourself for not "handling it better."

But what if the challenge is evidence
that you're stepping into something new?
What if it means you're stretching beyond the familiar,
and your system is simply adjusting?

No one is asking you to bypass your pain
or feel ashamed of it.
You need only honor it with curiosity.

Sometimes, the hardest moments come right before a breakthrough,
when your body and soul are asking,

Are you ready for this?
Can you stay with yourself through this?

When you shift how you relate to struggle,
you stop making it personal
and start making it transformational.

This isn't a test without purpose.
You are being invited
to meet yourself in a new way.

Self-Awareness: The Gateway to Change

If there's one truth at the heart of transformation, it's this:
You can't change what you aren't aware of.

Self-awareness is the doorway,
the beginning.

It's the moment you pause and realize,
Oh...this isn't who I want to be anymore.
This isn't mine to carry.
This is an old script, not a present truth.

The more you bring your patterns into the light,
the less power they hold over you.

Self-awareness is not the same as judgment.
It's the practice of noticing,
gently, honestly, and consistently.

It's observing when an old belief is driving your choices.
It's recognizing when a survival response is leading the
conversation—
and inviting your grounded, conscious self to take the lead instead.

What triggers us has the potential to teach us,
if we are open.
It was never going to be easy,
but it's illuminating all the same.

Ask yourself,
Is this my truth...or is this my programming?

Then choose, moment by moment,
what to keep,
what to release,
and what to rewrite.

Start small.

Tune in to your body, your breath, your reactions.
Where does tension show up?
What emotions rise in silence?
What thoughts play on loop when you're not trying to control
them?

Self-awareness gives you the map.
It won't solve everything,
but it will show you where you are.

And from there,
you get to choose where to go next.

This is the beginning of self-leadership.
You don't have all the answers yet,
but you're willing to ask better questions.

Expanding and Protecting Your Vital Life Force

Your energy is sacred.

It isn't just a vibe or a mood.
It's your life force,
the subtle current that flows through every part of your being,
emotionally, physically, mentally, spiritually.

This energy—known in different traditions as *prana*, *chi*, or *qi*—
is the foundation of your vitality,
your clarity,
and your capacity to create and connect.

When you're living in old patterns,
your energy contracts.

You may feel drained, foggy, reactive, or disconnected.
You may hold tension in your body that has no clear "reason."

That's your life force
trying to navigate around outdated beliefs and emotional residue.

But when you begin to release what no longer serves—
when you clear space
through self-awareness, nervous system care, and belief rewiring—
your energy begins to expand.

You feel lighter,
more present,
more available to yourself and others.
You're more *you*.

Your chakras—your body's energetic centers—play a key role here.

Each one governs a different aspect of your well-being.
When these centers are blocked or depleted,
it's often because energy is trying to move through an old program,
one that tells you to hide, overextend, shut down, or stay small.

But healing clears the channel.
Rewriting the code creates new space.

And the freer your energy flows,
the more capacity you have
to live aligned,
inspired,
and well.

This work extends beyond expanding your energy
into learning how to protect it.

As you grow,
you'll notice more clearly what depletes you:
people, habits, environments, even internal dialogue.

Boundaries—energetic, emotional, and physical—become essential.

Protecting your energy doesn't mean closing yourself off.
You only need to stay anchored in your truth
by choosing who and what gets access to your presence.

The more you honor your energy,
the more your energy will honor you.

The Role of Environment in Change

Healing doesn't happen in a vacuum.

Your growth is shaped
by more than what's happening inside of you;
it's also impacted
by what surrounds you.

If your environment reinforces the old version of you,
change will feel harder.

That's not to say it's impossible,
only that it will require more effort.

This is why it's so important
to consciously choose the spaces you inhabit:
- your physical surroundings,
- your relationships,
- your digital inputs,
- your daily rhythms,
- what you consume (food, media, conversations, beliefs).

All of it is information.
All of it is energy.
And all of it becomes part of your internal landscape.

Ask yourself,
Is my environment supporting my healing,
or is it pulling me back into patterns
I'm trying to release?

Sometimes a cluttered space
subtly reinforces overwhelm.

Sometimes a relationship
makes your growth feel like a threat.

Sometimes a routine
keeps you stuck in autopilot.

Small shifts can make a profound difference:
- Clear a space that feels stagnant.
- Add something beautiful or nourishing to your home.
- Allow time to be still, without producing or proving.
- Eat foods that support your clarity and strength.
- Be mindful of what you watch, read, and listen to.
- Create boundaries around draining conversations or content.
- Spend more time in nature.
- Surround yourself with people who honor your becoming.

Your nervous system takes cues from your environment.

When your space feels safe, spacious, or inspired,
you feel safer, too.

Again, you don't need to get this exactly right all the time.
It's all about alignment.

Curate a life that supports the person you're becoming,
and let go of the person you had to be.

Reframing Old Beliefs

Beliefs are not facts;
they are codes.
And codes can be rewritten.

The moment you recognize a belief as outdated or untrue,
you become the author again.

This is where the rewiring becomes intentional.

You start by noticing the belief:

I'm too much.
My needs are a burden.
Rest is lazy.
I have to earn love.

Then you ask,

Where did this come from?
Is it mine?
What has it cost me to keep believing this?

And slowly, courageously, you rewrite the code:

My presence is a gift.
My needs are sacred.
Rest is a form of love.
I don't have to earn love; I am already enough.

These aren't just affirmations.
They are acts of reclamation.

Each time you speak them, live them, practice them,
you build new pathways in your brain
and new possibilities in your life.

Reframing doesn't mean bypassing pain or pretending the past
didn't matter.
It means choosing what gets to lead your story now.

You're not erasing where you came from.
You're rewriting the code so your life reflects
your true, authentic self.

Celebrating Small Wins

Each aligned choice is worth celebrating.
Every act of intentional self-love is healing.
Tiny shifts
lead to lasting change.

Celebration, more than mere acknowledgment,
is a form of reinforcement.

It tells your brain,

Yes, this matters.
Yes, this is the new way.

Recognizing wins creates a positive feedback loop
that builds momentum
and strengthens trust.

It also softens the inner critic that says you should be further along.

So pause.
Notice.
Honor what's shifting.

Because small wins are the architecture of lasting change:

Taking a breath instead of lashing out.
Saying no without overexplaining.
Noticing a trigger and choosing to respond differently.
Allowing rest without guilt.
Speaking your truth, even if your voice trembles.

These moments matter. They are the everyday miracles of a rewired life.

They are evidence of new neural pathways being formed,
new energy moving,
and a new version of you emerging, quietly yet bravely.

When the Old Calls You Back

You cannot live fully in the new
while clinging to the old.

And as you change,
you will change your world:

your relationships,
your rhythms,
your sense of home.

Some will welcome it.
Others will resist.

Choose you anyway,
again
and again
and again.

Invitation

Before moving forward,
pause.
Let yourself arrive.

Breathe.
Feel your body.

Stretch.
Sway.
Be still.
Move.
Do whatever you need to.

Notice the quiet courage it takes to be here:
choosing awareness,
choosing growth,
choosing to come home to yourself.

This chapter has invited you to begin rewriting the code,
to loosen the grip of old beliefs,
to rewire your nervous system,
and to remember what has always been true:

You are not your past.
You are not your programming.

You are the one who gets to decide
what stays, what shifts, and what expands.

There's no rush,
only readiness.

Reflection Prompts

Create a space that feels safe and uninterrupted.
Bring your journal, a cup of tea, or anything that supports reflection.
Let this be sacred.
Let it be yours.

You may feel grounded.
You may feel stirred.
Both are welcome.

If overwhelm arises, pause.
Breathe.
Place your hand on your heart.
Ask gently,
What part of me is asking to be seen or supported?

You don't need to push through.
Just meet yourself where you are.

Inner Child and Inner Teenager

- What memories from childhood or adolescence feel connected to the patterns I'm working to reprogram?
- What did my younger self long to hear but never did? Can I offer those words now?
- In what ways are those younger parts of me still shaping how I move through the world today?

Shadow and Ego Work

- What emotions or desires have I been taught to suppress?
- When does my ego resist change? How does it try to keep me "safe"?
- How might I meet my shadow and ego with curiosity instead of judgment?

Energy and Releasing Old Programming

- How does my energy feel today, physically, emotionally, and spiritually?
- Where in my body do I feel tension, heaviness, or openness?
- What practices could help release stuck energy and reinforce new beliefs?

Neuroscience of Change and Reprogramming

- When was a time I successfully created change? What helped me stay consistent?
- What new belief am I ready to reinforce? How might I practice living it?
- What limiting belief has guided my life? Where did it originate?
- What empowering truth could I replace it with, and how would that feel in my body?

The Power of Patience and Self-Compassion
- Where am I still hard on myself for not being "healed enough"?
- How can I meet those parts with more grace?
- If I could speak to myself five years ago, what would I say?

Shifting Perspective on Challenges
- What challenge feels most alive for me right now? What might it be teaching me?
- What's one behavior or belief I'm ready to release?
- What would it feel like to live free from old programming?

Next Steps

Choose one area from the reflection prompts that stands out (inner child, energy, shadow work, etc.).

Write down a small, tangible action you can take this week.

Set an intention: *How will I nurture my reprogramming process this week?*

Celebrate your progress, whether it's a new awareness or a small act of self-honoring.

There is no such thing as too small.
Every aligned step counts.

Integration

Take a breath.
Let it anchor you.
Let it soften you.

Let it remind you of the truth:

You are not your programming.
You are not the roles you had to play,
the beliefs you inherited,
or the patterns you were taught to survive by.

You are the one who is choosing now,
the one who is awakening,
the one who is returning, layer by layer, to truth.

You are rewriting your story
with intention,
with compassion,
with courage.

And with every small, imperfect step,
you are growing in confidence.

Confidence doesn't come before the leap;
it comes because you dared to leap.

There's quiet magic in that,
the kind that reshapes worlds
from the inside out.

The past may have shaped you,
but it no longer defines you.

You are allowed to let go.
You are allowed to begin again.
You are allowed to become.

And you are already on your way.

CHAPTER 8

The Alchemy of Loss

"Grief does not change you, Hazel. It reveals you."
—John Green, *The Fault in Our Stars*

Where We've Been, Where We're Going

In Chapter 7,
we explored how old patterns shape us
and how the brain, body, and heart can rewire toward healing.
We remembered that transformation isn't a single leap;
it's small, intentional shifts
that ripple outward.

You don't have to repeat what was passed down.
You're allowed to begin again.

This chapter meets us at another threshold: the space loss creates.
Grief rearranges everything.
It exposes what matters most.
And in its wake, we're given a choice:
to collapse or to become.

Here, we explore the alchemy of loss—
not just the loss of loved ones,
but the quieter griefs, too:
the loss of a pet, a job, a relationship, or a sense of safety or identity.

Loss comes in many forms.
But each one, if we let it,
can become a portal to something deeper:
truth, clarity, and reclamation.

What We Grieve

Grief and loss are universal,
but they don't arrive in universal ways.

We grieve people,
but also places we've left behind,
futures that will never unfold,
childhoods we needed but never had,
and parts of ourselves we had to bury to survive.

Loss can feel like a shattering,
a rupture in what once felt whole.

Sometimes grief is loud, sharp, and immediate.
Sometimes it's quiet and delayed,
humming just beneath the surface
until something finally breaks it open.

Grief is the wave that follows loss.
It pulls us into memory, into meaning,
into all the places love once lived.

But grief doesn't only belong to love.
It echoes through the empty spaces.
And sometimes what we grieve
isn't what was, but what never was.

Grief shows us who we really are.
It strips us bare.

And in that nakedness,
we find what still lives beneath the rubble:
our capacity to rebuild,
our courage to become,
our willingness to carry both pain and possibility.

This chapter is about that becoming:
the grief that reshapes,
the loss that transforms,
the alchemy of what breaks us
and what we choose to create from it.

Loss as a Defining Thread

Loss showed up before I had language for it,
before I could name what was missing,
before I knew that what I was living was not what every child lived.

Loss has been one of my earliest teachers,
a thread woven through the fabric of my life.

Loss taught me the depths of sorrow,
the endurance of survival,
and the shape of resilience as something forged, not found.

And yet, even in the middle of all that loss,
there were moments of protection,
of subtle, divine guidance that I couldn't always see at the time,
but that I now recognize as part of what kept me going.

Grief, too, has marked every season of my life.
It didn't begin with the death of a person,
but with the absence of what every child deserves:
safety, presence, and care.

What follows in this chapter are glimpses.
I won't reveal every loss,
but I will share enough to show how deeply this thread runs
and the way it has shaped who I've become.

Childhood Loss and Identity

I didn't lose a parent in childhood.
But I lost something just as foundational:
the safety, nurture, and freedom that allow a child to grow into
themselves.

I lost what every child needs to thrive.

I lost safety.
I lost the freedom to explore, to rest, to breathe, to be held.

I lost the belief that the world is trustworthy and kind.

There was no consistent nurture,
no dependable rhythm,
no stable center.

Instead, there was violence,
emotional instability,
manipulation, control, and a house full of eggshells.

I learned early how to scan a room,
how to be quiet,
how to shape-shift,
how to become invisible or indispensable, depending on the day.

There wasn't space for my needs or my emotions.
So I buried them.

I became what the environment demanded:
the good girl, the helper, the high achiever,
the one who stayed two steps ahead of disaster.

That wasn't my personality;
it was my survival strategy.

And in that survival, I began to form an identity
from who I had to be to stay safe:

a people-pleaser,
a perfectionist,
a caretaker,
a high-functioning, emotionally starving child
who learned how to meet everyone else's needs
so she might not be punished for having her own.

It would take me years to recognize that
what had once passed for normal
was actually survival.

It would take me years to see that
what I carried wasn't mine to hold.

It would take me years to realize that I lost a childhood,
and that losing a childhood
can be just as devastating as losing a person.

The self that never got to be—

the version of me who got a healthy childhood—
must one day be grieved
before she can be reclaimed.

Loss of Innocence

Some losses are easy to name,
but that doesn't make them easy to carry.
And that doesn't make them any less significant.

A death,
a divorce,
a specific moment you can point to and say,
"That's when everything changed."

Some leave visible marks on the body.
Others leave invisible marks on the soul.
And many—especially those involving physical, emotional, sexual, or
spiritual abuse—leave both.

For me, the loss of innocence came in layers,
in a thousand small fractures,
each one chipping away at safety,
at trust,
at the belief that love could be unconditional.

I lived in a home where trauma was the norm
and abuse of all kinds was constant,
where faith was entangled with fear
and emotional instability and spiritual control shaped everything.

And some of those same patterns found me again, this time in
adulthood.

Just when I thought I had finally risen—
when I believed I had reclaimed my voice,
my body,
my boundaries,
my wholeness—
to the best of my ability,
with all the healing, growth, and clarity I had gathered...
I was raped.

By two different men at different times,
each claiming the name of Christ,
each using the language of God
to mask their harm.

The violence was sexual,
but it was also spiritual,
emotional,
and psychological.

It was a desecration wrapped in devotion.

I felt as if the toxic messages I had worked so hard to unravel—
obedience at all costs,
submission cloaked in Scripture,
disempowerment baptized as humility—
had found me again.

The lie that "goodness" could prevent harm
was shattered again.

In those moments, the echoes of my past became deafening.
The conditioning that told me to be small,
to be agreeable,
to be pleasing,
to be silent
all came rushing back.

The old scripts whispered,
See? It doesn't matter how strong you've become
or how much you've healed;
this is who you are meant to be.

But this time, I saw them for what they were:
lies.
And I didn't believe them.

Because this time, I knew the truth:
My voice is not wrong.
My no is not weakness.
The harm done to me is not mine to carry.
I was no longer the powerless child.
And I would not go back.

Even after all the growth,
even after reclaiming so much of myself,
there were still losses I could not outrun.

That doesn't make me less human, though;
it makes me braver.

I could have let the weight of it bury me.
I could have surrendered to the shame.
I could have decided that life wasn't worth living,
and no one would have blamed me.
It happens every day.

But something inside me knew there was more.

I am not unaffected.
I carry the scars.
Yet I keep coming back.

Some losses could have broken me entirely,
but I'm so glad they didn't.

Family Losses and Relationships

Beneath the layers of survival,
there was always a quiet strength,
a flicker,
a pulse,
a persistent ember that refused to go out.

It carried me through every heartbreak,
every dark night of the soul.

And I've had more than one.

I lost many of the people I loved,
each in their own way,
each carving something from my heart.

My maternal grandparents were emotionally distant.
I spent years trying to earn the approval of my grandfather,
craving his attention,
longing for approval I never received.

His harsh greetings and rigid standards
only mirrored the unmet needs I had learned to normalize.

My paternal grandparents were more present,
but their presence brought its own disconnection:
a mix of warmth and neglect,
of showing up and disappearing,
that left its mark on my understanding of relationships and identity.

There was love in my extended family.
But there was also silence,
avoidance,
a lack of protection,
and emotional withholding.

It left me questioning myself,
wondering what was real,
what was earned,
and whether love had to be chased to be kept.

Even in family,
grief and belonging often coexisted.

Connection was conditional.
And affection was never quite safe.

Brother, Hero

My brother was, in many ways, like a father figure to me:
protective,
adoring,
generous,
kind,
a natural leader,
my hero.

He saw me,
looked out for me,
loved me without condition or confusion.

Both of my siblings left home early,
and even then, I knew
freedom was a kind of safety.

I remember the night he decided to run.
His room was dark, the window cracked open.
He had whispered his plan to me quietly
with that look in his eyes:
part fear, part hope.

I gathered what I could:
a shirt, jeans, maybe socks.
I laid them out for him like an offering,
just beneath the windowsill.

Helping him leave felt like the most loving act possible.
I wanted him to get out,
to be free.

But once he was gone,
a new kind of silence settled in.
The house felt even more unstable without him.
I had helped him escape...
but I was still there.

I was too young to leave,
yet old enough to understand
what I had just lost.

In 1993, just two months after I got married,
he died in an alcohol-related motorcycle accident.

He was only twenty-nine.
And just like that,
he was gone.

The grief was more than sibling grief;
it was paternal, foundational.
It left a raw, unfillable space,
a void that echoed through every part of me.

I cried every single day for over a year.
I thought the pain was going to kill me.

I remember the moment I found out:
The police called me in the middle of the night.
I was the one who had to call my mother.

When she answered,
I told her what had happened.
Her immediate response—sharp and guttural—was
"What a waste of a life."

I know that was her pain speaking.
I know she loved her son deeply.
But the weight of those words has never fully left me.

Even now, I sometimes wonder,
Who says that?
And then I remember:
someone in pain,
someone grieving,
someone whose emotions are so often filtered through hurt and
bluntness.

Over time, I've come to feel my brother's presence
as something soft and steady,
like a quiet force walking beside me
through every hard season,
still leading,
still watching over me.

Held in Silence

In 2002,
I experienced a miscarriage.

It shook me in a way I didn't expect.
I instinctively felt it was a boy.

And I've often wondered
if he and my brother walk together now,
watching over me
and the life I've built
from the pieces of what I've lost.

I had already spent seven years
navigating infertility and heartbreak.
My first daughter was just two years old.
And still,
this loss hollowed me in a different way.

The truth is,
I felt deeply alone for the entirety of my marriage.
But this loss magnified it.
The silence around my grief
was louder than any words.

There was no space for sorrow,
only survival.

So I tucked it away,
like so many women do.

It took me decades to fully process that miscarriage,
to even admit how much it mattered.

Later, I began to reflect,
to feel,
to open.

I turned again to God
and to spirituality
to make sense of the loss.

And in return, I received insight,
new beginnings,
and hope.

That was the first time I allowed myself
to see the loss as something more than pain:
a kind of soul invitation,
a reminder
that even in the emptiness,
something sacred remains.

I carry him with me still,
not only in memory,
but in meaning.

What Would Never Be

When my marriage ended—
separation in 2003,
divorce finalized in 2005—
it wasn't just the loss of a relationship.

It was the loss of a dream,
a vision I had clung to
with all the hope and effort I could muster.

I had built that dream slowly and intentionally
in an effort
to rewrite the past.

I wanted to create a home filled with warmth,
with presence,
with the kind of love
I never got to fully experience growing up.

And for a time,
I believed I could with him.

I poured myself into trying
to build something lasting,
into being everything I thought a partner should be.

But over time,
what I hoped for began to slip further away.

It wasn't a single catastrophic collapse,
but a gradual erosion of connection
over years of being unseen
and unmet.

Eventually, I came to understand why:
This vision I'd been holding
was mine alone.

The love I longed to create
wasn't something we could build together.

So when it ended,
it didn't shatter me
in a sudden way.

I had already grieved
so much of what was missing
while still inside the marriage.

But it was still a loss,
and a deep one.

The pain wasn't just in what had happened;
it was in everything that would now never happen.

Holidays.
Rituals.
Shared laughter in the kitchen.

The soft, ordinary moments
of building a life together.

Gone.

The grief was layered.
It was the death of a marriage,
but also the death of my vision of family:
a safe, loving unit.

I had worked,
to the best of my ability,
to create that.

But now,
it would never be.

It wasn't just the end of a relationship.
It was the quiet extinguishing
of a hope I had carried for so long:
the hope that I could redeem the past
by building something new.

And yet,
I know the loss wasn't mine alone.

There was loss for my ex-husband, too,
in the time shared with his daughters.

And there was loss for my daughters:
in the absence of an intact family,

in the shift of what "home" would now mean,
in the memories that would look different
than the ones I had hoped they'd carry.

There was also the toll of accumulated time spent traveling
every other weekend across the state,
a rhythm we all endured
in the name of maintaining connection.

And with time,
I began to see it as a gift.

That's not to say it didn't hurt,
but it also set me on a path
toward deeper healing,
toward wholeness.

It pushed me toward the kind of life
that could only be born
from the ashes of that dream.

Difficult as it's been,
I believe it has all unfolded—
and will continue to unfold—
for everyone's highest good.

My Sister's Daughter

In 2012,
my niece died unexpectedly at just thirty years old.

It was an accidental death,
a tragic moment
that shattered the center of my sister's world
and sent our entire family into another wave of grief.

She was more than my niece.
She carried my first name as her middle name,
a small detail that always felt like an honor.
I had been proud to be an aunt since I was thirteen.
In many ways,
I'd felt like I was growing up alongside her.

I always wanted to be a steady presence in her life.
And while I sometimes felt I was falling short,
the love I had for her never wavered.

When she died,
I remember thinking,
How does one family endure so much?
How can both my mother and my sister
bear the loss of an adult child?

In a different way,
I, too, had lost a child, through miscarriage.
Though the experiences were not the same,
the ache was familiar.

My niece left behind a son,
just five months younger than my youngest daughter.

He is growing into an extraordinary young man:
kind,
grounded,
resilient.

In him,
I see so much of her,
and yet he is entirely his own.
He is shaped by love and loss,
but not defined by it.

Though her death added another chapter
to a life already touched by sorrow,
I hold on to the light she left behind
and the way it still shines through him
and through all of us who love her.

Grieving What Never Was

In 2017,
I lost my father
on my oldest daughter's seventeenth birthday.

True to form,
even in passing,
he managed to center someone else's moment around himself.

It was bittersweet,
a milestone celebration wrapped in mourning,
laughter braided with heaviness,
a glimpse of my family's graceful resilience.

His death brought relief in many ways.

By that time,
I had long been processing and grieving our relationship.

I loved him,
yet I didn't feel close to him.
I didn't feel safe.

The grief wasn't just for his absence.
It was for the father I never truly had,
the one I needed,
the one who'd never existed—and now never would.

He was intelligent,
a skilled architect.

He functioned in the world just enough
to make people believe things were fine.

But inside our home, it was chaotic,
stressful,
unpredictable,
frightening.

His behavior was erratic and volatile,
emotionally unstable,
socially unaware,
violent at times,
rarely regulated,
never present in the ways that mattered.

He stole innocence and safety from his children.

Some of the trauma was overt.
Some of it was wrapped in silence and secrecy.
But all of it shaped us.

We lived in a state of chronic fear, confusion, hypervigilance, and
tension.

I don't remember much of my childhood.
And what I do remember is mostly pain:

control,
codependency,
suppressed or fragmented memories,
dissociation.

I was dysregulated, but composed,
well-behaved,
high-functioning.
I was trained to be agreeable,
trained to survive.

My chronic physical pain began around age nineteen,
pain I now know was the embodiment
of everything I had no space to speak.

And threaded through it all was religious trauma.

God was used as a threat,
shame as a tool,
love as a condition.

We were taught to fear punishment,
to obey without question,
to view ourselves as inherently broken.

There was no room for self-worth,
no room for love.

The Mother I Cared For

In March of 2025,
I lost my mother.

Her passing opened a different kind of grief:
more layered, more complex.

I was her official caregiver in the final years of her life.
But the truth is,
I had been offering her care my entire life.

From childhood through adulthood,
I tended to her emotions,
absorbed her pain,
and tried to make her feel okay.

There's one moment from my childhood I'll never forget:
They were fighting, again.
He was driving.
She opened the car door to jump out while it was still moving.

And from the back seat,
I reached forward and grabbed her,
held her back from leaving,
from disappearing,
from dying.

I was only a child.
But I had already learned
that keeping her alive
might depend on me.

It was only in the later years
that the caretaking became visible to others.
But for me, it had always been there.

I stayed by her side
as she left this world.
I sang to her.
I was touching her when she passed.
And I walked her to the edge
of what comes next.

She was the parent who showed affection,
who sometimes called me Angel Annie—
if I was measuring up.

She taught me what care could look like.
But love from her came with strings attached.

She was charming,
funny,
creative,
energetic,
magnetic.

But she could turn on a dime:
from warmth to criticism,
from praise to punishment,
from calling me "Angel Annie" to "Gruesome Gertie."

I was attuned to her moods,
trained to meet her needs,
trained to disappear into her emotional tides.

She made me her substitute spouse.
That dynamic, so common, so confusing, blurred everything.

It taught me that my role was to soothe her,
to stabilize her,
to give her what no one else would.
And I did.

Because even though I did matter,
I'd learned it was safer
to believe I didn't,
to act as if she mattered much more.

There was also a deeper truth I've had to reckon with:
She prioritized her husband, my father, above all else.

Even when she was miserable.
Even when he was clearly unstable and unsafe.

She chose loyalty to that relationship
over protection of and safety for her children.

Yes, there were a few late-night escapes to a hotel,
but we always came back—
and the chaos always returned:

the screaming,
the hitting,
the breaking,
the fear.

It was all a never-ending loop of violence and denial.

She knowingly allowed us to remain in that environment
with a man who was deeply disturbed
and dangerous in every way.

Seeing Her Clearly

After my father passed,
I began to see my mother more clearly.

For much of my life, it was easy to view her
as the helpless one,
the victim,
the fragile woman
trying to survive his volatility.

She was petite, physically small,
and that made me feel even more protective of her.
I felt like I had to shield her,
like her pain was bigger than mine.

But once he was gone,
something shifted.

Now that he was no longer casting the largest shadow,
hers came into focus.

And what I saw
shook me.

I began to recognize her own "monster-like" traits:
the screaming,
the emotional volatility,
the instability that erupted in ways I had once dismissed.

She had hit my father,
thrown things,

fought back—
and yet, somehow, I had only ever seen her
as the one needing protection.

I realized how much of her harm
I had normalized.

It forced me to re-evaluate everything I thought I understood
about our dynamic,
about her,
about me.

Caring for someone who contributed to your pain
complicates everything:

grief,
boundaries,
self-worth.

The lines get tangled
between love and harm,
between presence and survival,
between what was given
and what was never safe to receive.

She was wounded, too,
loyal to a fault,
impressionable,
codependent,
often anxious and depressed.

She was deeply shaped by her own unmet needs
and the pedestal she placed men on.

Both of my parents were deeply wounded,
dysregulated,
neurodivergent in different but overlapping ways.

They were seekers of truth,
but they rarely found peace.

There were no boundaries in our home,
no modeling of self-love,
no emotional safety,
no spaciousness to process,
to question,
to simply be.

Even among siblings,
while there was love,
there was also comparison,
invalidation,
and survival-mode roles
we didn't choose but had to inhabit.

I grieve my parents,
and I grieve the childhood my siblings and I could have had.

Grief is a complicated emotion
born of love and loss.

Yet not all loss is rooted in love.

Sometimes we grieve what never was,
what could have been,
what should have been.

We feel the absence of safety,
the betrayal of trust,
the cost of having to grow up too fast.

I grieve all of that, too.

What I Choose to Carry

Now, with both of my parents gone,
I've become the oldest living generation in my family.

It feels strange...
yet also liberating.

There's grief in it,
but also a widening sense of space.

It's a quiet shift in lineage
that I am still learning how to hold.

I hope my parents are free now,
held in a love they never fully accessed here,
known and whole in a way they never were in human form.

I've felt my mother's presence since she passed:
in sunsets,
in quiet moments,
in colors that seem more vivid than they used to.

I'm grateful for the life they gave me,
for the breath I carry,
for the chance to do it differently.

I continue to grieve,
to integrate,
to heal.

And I move forward,
not with bitterness,
but with reverence,
boundaries,
and love.

I am both a continuation of what was
and the beginning of what can be.

Loss of My Friend

In 2020,
on my birthday,
I lost one of my dearest friends
to a serious illness she had been battling.

It was the kind of loss
that doesn't always come with ceremony
but that leaves a permanent indentation
in the heart.

She wasn't family by blood,
but she was family by soul.

Her presence was patient,
grounded,
safe.

She made space for me,
for my processing,
for my silence,
for my truth.

She understood me
even when I didn't have words.
And she never asked me to explain myself
to be loved.

Her timing was profound:
She died on the same day of the year I was born.

And that's a strange thing,
to carry celebration and sorrow
in the same breath.

I still feel her sometimes:
in small moments,
in the quiet,
in the way I care for others now.

Her loss reminded me
that not all families are given.
Some are chosen.
And some leave
before you're ready to let them go.

But love remains.

And the imprint of being known,
of being truly seen,
never fades.

Unlike the losses I experienced in my family,
this one wasn't tangled in pain.
It didn't ask me to untangle
love from harm,
presence from betrayal.

There was no confusion,
only grief,
clean and sacred.

In the stillness that followed,
something softened in me:
a sense of being held,
even in the ache
of letting go.

Spiritual Resilience and Healing

Through every loss, there was one thing that never completely left
me,
and that was my connection with God.

It wasn't always clear.
It wasn't always strong.
But it never disappeared.
Even in my loneliest seasons, I knew I was being held.

Sometimes it felt like a fragile thread, just enough to keep me
tethered.
Other times, it was the only thing that made sense in a world that
didn't.

I trusted God, so I knew that what those men did,
those who used God's name to control and harm,
was not a reflection of God's love.
It was a reflection of human failure.

God did not abandon me.

Their abuse did not reflect God's love.
Their silence did not reflect God's voice.
Their hypocrisy did not reflect the truth of who I know Him to be.

My connection with God remains unbroken,
not because of them,
but despite them.

God's love carried me through the darkest nights
of pain, abuse, loss, and grief.
And I emerged stronger each time,
knowing that this love would always prevail,
even when the people who claimed to serve God failed miserably.

Still, my relationship with God had to be reclaimed.
I needed to release the fear
and the doctrine
so I could find Him through presence,
intimacy,
and trust instead.

It didn't grow in cathedrals.
It grew in silence,
in nature,
in whispered prayers,
in the breath between sobs.

It grew in the subtle ways I was reminded
that I mattered
and that hope always existed, no matter how much I lost.

Even now, my faith isn't something I perform.
It's something I live.
It's sacred,
relational,
alive.

And that has made all the difference.

Even After Everything

The journey to reclaim my sense of self,
safety,
and trust
has not been linear.

It's been layered,
tender,
messy,
sacred.

Every loss I've named here—
and every one I haven't—
left its imprint.
But it also shaped something new in me:

a depth,
a capacity,
a kind of wisdom
that only emerges when you've walked through fire
and kept your heart open.

There were seasons when I felt utterly abandoned,
facing life's challenges with nothing but my faith
and a fierce determination to create a better future
for my children and for myself.

Yet, through all of it,
often feeling as though I was navigating life alone,
I raised two beautiful daughters.

Grief and loss were among my greatest teachers.
I learned much, not from what they took,
but from what they revealed.

They showed me the dual nature of life:
how pain and beauty,
despair and hope,
can exist side by side.

Each loss etched a space within me,
and in time, those spaces were filled
with unexpected gifts:
compassion,
wisdom,
and a deeper reverence for the present moment.

I also recognize the beliefs I once carried:
that I was alone and unsupported,
that any help that came
would be inconsistent or incomplete,
that it was all on me.

I sometimes wonder how differently
I might have navigated my losses
if I had been more healed,
more aware,
more held.

But I also hold deep gratitude
for every version of myself who carried me here:

the one who kept going,
the one who did her best,
the one who chose to believe
that healing was possible.

These experiences shaped me,
but they did not define me.

What defined me
was how I chose to respond.

It was how I kept reaching for the light
when the darkness tried to settle in.

It was how I decided, again and again,
to trust in healing,
to trust in love,
to trust in myself.

I carry the weight of these moments.
But I also carry the strength,
the resilience,
the clarity,
and the self-trust
that have allowed me to rise again and again.

My faith is now
more than a performance
or a rulebook;
it's a lived experience
of divine love and grace.

It was born not in spite of my pain,
but because of what I've found within it.

Even after everything,
I still believe in goodness.
I still believe in kindness.
I still believe in love.
And I still believe that dreams can come true.

Support in Loss and Living

Grief has cracked me open repeatedly.
And inside each opening,
there was more light revealed.

The light was within me,
but it was also coming into me from sources all around me:

the ever-present love of God,
the quiet guidance of angels,
the soft imprint of those who have gone before me.

Much of the light is in the sacred, ordinary support I encounter every
single day:
- the person who holds the door for me at the store;
- the friend who meets me for a walk;
- the trees, flowers, stars, sun, and clouds
  that witness my becoming;
- the healers who offer safe touch, presence, and compassion,
  reminding my body and spirit that I am whole;
- the spaces and souls who hold me gently in my becoming,
  through conversation, creativity, and care;
- the mentors and guides who help me
  remember the truth of who I am;
- the community who sees me, supports
  me, and walks alongside me,
  even from afar;
- the books that find me when I need them,
  podcasts that remind me I'm not alone,
  and music that helps me put myself back together again.

Living with Grief, Healing Through Loss

Grief isn't something to overcome;
it's something we learn to live with.

Throughout these stories,
we've seen how grief emerges not only from death,
but from the loss of what was,
what should have been,
or what we hoped would last.

We've explored how grief lives in the body,
in memory,
in the space between love and pain.

And we've remembered that healing doesn't require forgetting.
It requires presence,
compassion,
and a willingness to feel.

When we choose to honor grief,
we don't just survive loss;
we begin to be transformed by it.

Recognizing the Many Faces of Loss

What's often missed about grief
is that it doesn't only rise from death.

Grief shows up
whenever something we once counted on
is no longer there.

When we learn to recognize its forms,
we can begin to hold it with compassion.

These are some of the most common, yet often overlooked,
faces of grief:

Loss of a loved one:
sudden or expected, bringing sadness, longing, and identity shifts

End of a relationship:
romantic, familial, or platonic; grief for what was hoped for,
imagined, or invested in

Divorce or separation:
loss of partnership, shared dreams, and family rhythm

Illness or diagnosis (your own or a loved one's):
loss of safety in the body or future plans

Miscarriage or infertility:
a deeply personal and often invisible grief

Career or job loss:
loss of identity or purpose

Unfulfilled dreams or life transitions:
letting go of who you thought you'd become

Loss of innocence or trust:
trauma, betrayal, or spiritual crisis

Relocation or identity shifts:
moving, changing roles, or evolving spiritually

Cumulative grief:
when layered losses accumulate without space to heal

Grief is as unique as the person experiencing it.
And so is healing.

Healing Grief and Trauma Beyond Memory

Not all trauma is stored in words.

Many memories live in the body,
in the places we tighten,
in the spaces we hold our breath,
in the way we shrink, freeze, or overextend
without even realizing it.

Some wounds have no clear timeline.
They don't live in language.
They live in patterns,
in posture,
in the nervous system's quiet alerts.

You don't have to remember everything
to begin releasing what was never yours to carry.

Deep wounds—
from lost innocence, betrayal, and shattered trust
to the quiet erosion of hope,
the absence of dreams fulfilled,
and the sudden loss of loved ones—
leave their mark on the body and soul.

But healing becomes possible when we listen instead of trying to
"get over it."

Healing happens when we offer the body what it was once denied:
safety,
presence,
and compassion.

Transformation begins in small, sacred ways:
- in the trembling of a body that once held still to survive;
- in the deep breath that wasn't safe to take before;
- in the yawning that opens space, the shaking that releases old fear, and the stretching that welcomes life back in;
- in the tears that come without warning;
- in the laughter that reminds us joy still lives here.

Every act of expression,
movement, breath, creativity, and surrender
becomes a powerful step toward reclaiming life.

And healing doesn't happen by accident.
It has to be nurtured, supported, and intentionally embodied.

Practices to Support Your Healing Journey

If you're ready to support your body, heart, and nervous system through grief and trauma, here are some gentle pathways:

- **Nervous System Regulation:**
  This can be breathwork, grounding techniques, cold water exposure (if that works for your nervous system), or vagal nerve stimulation.
  These practices help shift your physiological state, bringing your body back to safety and balance when stress, anxiety, or old survival patterns arise.

  Grounding can be as simple as feeling your feet on grass,
  holding a warm mug with both hands,
  or placing a hand on your heart.
  It's a way to come home to your body,
  to remember you are here, and you are safe.

- **Somatic Movement and Body-Based Healing:**
  Gentle practices like yoga, intuitive walking, body scanning, stretching, shaking, or dancing
  invite your body to release stored tension
  and express what words often cannot.

  They reconnect you to your inner rhythms,
  your breath,
  and your physical presence.

  Intuitive walking is simple but sacred:
  walking without a set path or pace,
  letting your body lead

while tuning in to sensations,
such as the earth beneath your feet
and the quiet wisdom within.

Body scanning is a practice of presence:
bringing awareness through your body
from head to toe,
noticing what you feel,
where you hold tension,
and what softens with attention.

These practices whisper,
You don't have to think your way to healing.
You can feel your way there.

- **Mindfulness and Meditation:**
  These are simple moments of presence without judgment,
  practices that invite you to stay with what is, breathe
  through it, and witness your experience with compassion.

- **Creative Expression:**
  Practice journaling, art, or music, allowing your inner truth
  to move outward into form and feeling.

- **Music and Sound Healing:**
  Listening to frequency tones, grounding playlists, soul-
  nourishing songs, or music that supports emotional release,
  integration, or peace can be a powerful part of healing.

Some frequencies are believed to carry specific benefits:
396 Hz may help release fear and guilt,

while 528 Hz, often called the "love frequency," is associated with heart healing and transformation.

One study even found that listening to music tuned to 528 Hz lowers stress hormones and increases markers of relaxation and emotional well-being more than standard music tuning.[6]

You can explore the wider world of sound healing or simply trust what resonates and soothes your spirit. Whether it's a specific tone or a song that feels like home, let the sound meet you where you are.

- **Nature Therapy and Simple Rituals:**
  Spend time outside,
  touch your bare feet on the earth,
  plant something to honor loss or let go.
  Let awe find you in the sunlight through trees, the persistence of a bloom, or the whisper of the wind reminding you, *You belong.*

- **Connection and Community:**
  Find safe spaces where you can be witnessed without needing to perform, explain, or fix anything.
  Healing often begins in being seen—even silently.

---

6 **Kaho Akimoto et al.,** "Effect of 528 Hz Music on the Endocrine System and Autonomic Nervous System," *Health* 10, no. 9 (2018): 1159–1170, https://doi. org/10.4236/health.2018.109088.

This might look like
- sending a voice note to a trusted friend who lets you share authentically, who listens, and who lets *you* decide if you just want to be heard or if you'd like input.
- being a part of a community that aligns with your values and goals.

True connection meets you where you are—and stays with you throughout your journey.

There is no one right way to heal.
These are simply invitations to find what works for you.

You do not need to recall every detail
to release the weight of grief and trauma.

The body knows.
And the body also knows how to heal.

There is always a way forward.

And while the path toward healing may not always feel easy,
staying trapped in the past
is far more exhausting.

Each movement, each breath,
each moment of creative expression
brings you closer to the freedom and light
that has always lived within you.

You have already begun healing.
Every small act of care,
every time you choose you from self-love,
every moment of awareness is a seed planted.
Trust that your healing is unfolding, even when you cannot see it yet.

Invitation

Before you dive into these reflections,
give yourself a moment to arrive.

Pause.
Breathe.
Notice your body.

Let yourself move if you need movement,
or find stillness if you need stillness.

Take a few deep, grounding breaths.
Stretch.
Shake out your hands.
Place your feet flat against the floor or earth.

Feel yourself supported.

If you'd like,
get a glass of water, a cup of tea, or a nourishing snack.

Find a comfortable place to sit,
either with a journal and pen
or your computer, whichever feels easier.

This is your time.
This is your space.

Let these reflections meet you where you are,
without judgment, without rush,
with the same compassion you are learning to offer yourself.

Keep a journal, or simply allow these questions to live inside you as a quiet guide.

When you're ready, explore the reflections below at your own pace.

Reflection Prompts

- Which losses—recent or long ago—have impacted you most deeply?
- What has been the emotional landscape of that grief?
- What parts of you are still holding the grief?
  Is there a younger version of you—an inner child or teen—who never got to fully feel or express the pain?
  Does the adult version of you try to hold it all together, even now?
  Pause and notice:
  Who inside of you is still carrying the weight?
  What do they need?
- In what ways has trauma shaped your relationship to grief?
- How has it affected your ability to feel, express, or be witnessed in pain?
- Were there moments in your life that felt like "too much," moments that were never named as trauma but that still live in your nervous system or body memory?
- How do you care for yourself when grief or trauma resurfaces?
- What supports you in returning to presence and self-compassion?
- What version of you still needs permission to grieve or rest?
- Where does grief live in your body right now?
- What sensations do you notice (tightness, holding, pressure, numbness, heat)?
- If your body could speak, what might it say? What might it ask for?

- What beliefs have you carried about grief or pain?
- Were you taught that emotions make you weak or that grief has an expiration date?
- Are there quiet narratives you're ready to release?
- Where in your life does unprocessed grief still linger? Explore this by tuning in to moments that still feel heavy, unexplained, or unfinished.
  Notice where you brace, go silent, or feel disconnected.
  These may be the places inviting deeper healing.

Integration

Take a breath.
Let it soften you.
Let it remind you of the truth:

You don't have to rush this.
You are allowed to grieve slowly,
to feel deeply,
to not have the words.

You are not too much.
You are not too late.
You are not alone.

This part of your story is sacred,
because even though it's not easy,
you are showing up anyway.

Even now,
even here,
healing is happening.

This, too, is part of your becoming.

CHAPTER 9

Wholehearted and Wise

"To be fully seen by somebody, then, and be loved anyhow—this is a
human offering that can border on miraculous."
—Elizabeth Gilbert

Where We've Been, Where We're Going

In Chapter 8, we explored the many faces of grief and the ways loss
shapes us.
We honored the alchemy that happens when we let pain speak,
when we let it soften us instead of harden us.
We made space for the truths we've carried,
the wounds we've outgrown,
and the light that still finds its way through the cracks.
Grief revealed what we had to release.

Now, we turn toward what we're ready to reclaim.

This chapter is about reinhabiting the fullness of who we are. We'll explore how wisdom emerges from our willingness to feel, how wholeheartedness begins with the brave act of self-honoring, and how healing invites us to live with more intention, integrity, and joy.

We'll reflect on the courage it takes to live from the inside out and what it means to choose wholeness as our way forward.

Foundations of Wholeness

We all long for connection,
to be known, seen, and loved,
not for what we do,
but for who we are.

And yet, so often, we hide
behind roles,
behind fear,
behind the need to be enough.

The path back to our truest selves
asks us to move through four sacred gateways:

Authenticity is where we begin: the remembering of who we are
underneath it all.
Vulnerability is how we let ourselves be seen: messy, real, human.
Trust gives us the courage to keep showing up, even when it's hard.
Discernment offers the wisdom to know what's safe, aligned, and
true.

Together, they become the compass,
guiding us out of self-abandonment
and into the grounded, open-hearted life we desire.

But a compass is only useful
if we have a vessel to carry us forward.

That vessel is **graceful resilience**.

Graceful resilience is what holds us steady
as we navigate the unknown.
You are doing more than surviving now;
you are honoring every version of you that already has:
your inner child,
who kept hope alive;
your teenage self,
who carried feelings without language;
your adult self,
who keeps choosing growth, even when it's hard.

Graceful resilience is built
in strength,
but also in softness and surrender.
It comes from choosing rest over exertion,
truth over performance.

Take a moment
to say to your past self,

I see how hard you tried.
I see how strong you were.
I'll take it from here.

You no longer have to fight to be worthy.
You already are.

Let this chapter be your compass and your ship,
a gentle guide for the journey home to yourself.

Together, we'll walk through authenticity, vulnerability, trust,
and discernment
as more than ideas:
as embodied ways of living.

You are worthy of a life
that reflects your truth.

Let's begin.

The Long Road to Inner Trust

When I began my journey in my twenties,
I didn't have language for authenticity, vulnerability, trust, or discernment,
at least not in a way that translated to my relationships,
especially the one I had with myself.

My upbringing and early programming
instilled a different kind of logic,
one in which love was earned,
emotions were hidden,
and survival came before truth.

And yet, something in me still longed for more.

So I began reading, journaling, learning in every way I could.
I attended therapy.
I asked hard questions.
I kept showing up.

I'm proud of the younger me:
hungry to learn
and courageous enough
to take those first uncertain steps
into something better.

Those early steps often felt small,
more like failures than breakthroughs.
But I held on to the belief that change was possible.

And every promise I made to myself,
every book I read,
every tool I practiced
became the foundation
for the strength and clarity I carry now.

But more than anything,
I started listening
to my body,
to my gut,
to the quiet voice inside that said,
There is more for you.
You are not broken.
You already know the way.

That voice was sometimes my inner child,
asking to be heard.
Sometimes my higher self,
whispering truth through the static.
Sometimes just a feeling I couldn't explain...
but knew I couldn't ignore.

I devoured books.
In the early years, these were just some of them:
- *Safe People* by Dr. Henry Cloud and Dr. John Townsend
- *Boundaries* by Dr. Henry Cloud and Dr. John Townsend
- *Codependent No More* by Melody Beattie
- *How To Go On Living When Someone You Love Dies* by Dr. Therese A. Rando

Each one gave me language for what I had lived
and a glimpse of what was possible.
They helped me understand patterns, trauma, grief, and boundaries
in a way I had never been taught.

Later, I found other books that deepened my self-awareness
and offered tools for emotional, spiritual, and nervous system
healing:

- *Toxic Faith* by Stephen Arterburn and Jack Felton
- *The Gifts of Imperfection* by Dr. Brené Brown
- *How to Do the Work* by Dr. Nicole LePera
- *The Alchemist* by Paulo Coelho
- *Switch On Your Brain* by Dr. Caroline Leaf
- *Mutant Message Down Under* by Marlo Morgan

And over time, the list continued to grow.
These books didn't just teach me;
they met me
in grief,
in growth,
in moments of unraveling and becoming.

But knowledge alone wasn't enough.
The real challenge was applying it,
especially when the only compass I had
was the one I was just beginning to trust:
my own.

The Pillars of Wholehearted Living

To live wholeheartedly is to live awake,
to show up as your true self,
rooted in your values,
clear in your energy,
open to love,
and safe within your own skin.

There's no need for performance.
This is a practice,
a moment-by-moment return to truth.

It's a beautiful and real way to live.

And it begins with four foundational principles:
authenticity, vulnerability, trust, and discernment.

Authenticity: The Return to Truth

Authenticity is not something you find outside of yourself.
It's who you are beneath the noise:
before the roles,
before the masks,
before the programming told you who you had to be.

It's the brave act of honoring your values,
your feelings,
and your needs,
even when it's uncomfortable.

Living authentically doesn't mean you never feel fear.
It means you no longer let fear make your decisions.
It asks you to tell the truth—
first to yourself,
then to the world—
in ways that feel safe and aligned.

Authenticity isn't about being flawless;
it's about being real.
And for me, it began in the quiet unraveling of a marriage.

I had been the peacemaker, the fixer, the one who made things
better.
But beneath all the effort and accommodation, I had abandoned
myself.
My authenticity returned as a whisper:
This isn't who I am. This isn't what I want.
It was the first thread I dared to pull.

Vulnerability: The Courage to Be Seen

Vulnerability is not weakness.
It is your strength in motion.
It's choosing to be seen,
especially when your programming tells you not to be your true self,
when everything in you wants to make everything better...
or just disappear.

It's the willingness to say,
This is who I am.
This is what I need.
This is what matters to me.

During that season, I let a few trusted people see behind the curtain.
I admitted I was exhausted, lonely, unseen.
I let the tears fall.
I told the truth out loud:
"This isn't love, at least not the kind I want anymore."

Vulnerability invited connection.
No one "fixed" the problem,
but I was no longer alone.

Trust: Building Safety Within and With Others

Trust is the foundation of healthy relationships,
not just with others, but with yourself.
It's the belief that your needs matter,
that your intuition is wise,
and that your voice is worth hearing.

In those early days of waking up to my truth,
I didn't feel ready.
But I started small.
I began to trust the signals in my body,
the knowing in my gut,
the ache in my heart.
I promised myself,
I will not abandon me.
I will not stay small to stay safe.

Trust grew each time I honored what I knew to be true,
even when it would've been easier to dismiss or delay.

Trust is earned
not by doing everything right,
but by consistently showing up.
You don't demand it;
you build it,
moment by moment,
choice by choice.

Discernment: Knowing What's True for You

Discernment is the quiet wisdom that guides when and how to share
your truth.
It's the voice that whispers, *Not everyone gets access to all of you.*

Discernment may seem like closing your heart,
but it's merely a way to protect your energy.
It helps you identify red flags, honor your gut,
and choose spaces and people that feel emotionally safe.

Eventually, discernment showed me the exit,
not in anger, but in clarity.
I stopped overexplaining.
I stopped trying to earn understanding from someone who couldn't
meet me where I was.
I knew what I had to do.
So I walked away.

Discernment teaches you to slow down,
to pause,
to listen,
to move in alignment instead of urgency.

It allows you to honor your vulnerability
without handing it to those who haven't earned your trust.

Returning to Graceful Resilience

If the four pillars—
authenticity, vulnerability, trust, and discernment—
make up the compass that guides you home to yourself,
then graceful resilience is the vessel that carries you forward.

It's the reminder that you are made for more than surviving what life
brings,
that you are allowed to soften when you want to harden,
to rest when the world demands performance,
and to choose love when fear resurfaces.

It's built in the quiet moments
when you honor your truth,
hold your boundaries,
and still keep your heart open.

Graceful resilience doesn't rush the process;
it trusts it.

Touchstones of Truth

The journey toward wholehearted living begins with awareness
and unfolds through small, honest steps.

Below are simple invitations to deepen your connection
with each of the four pillars:
authenticity, vulnerability, trust, and discernment.

You can explore these prompts through journaling, stillness,
movement, or quiet thought.
Let them guide you without pressuring you.

At the end of each section, you'll find a gentle affirmation:
a phrase you can speak, write, or reflect on as a way to shift your
inner dialogue.

Think of them not as magic words,
but as kind reminders:
words of truth to return to when old patterns rise up.

1. Authenticity
Reflection:
- What feels most real and true in me right now?
- Where am I still performing or hiding, and why?

    Affirmation:
    I let go of who I thought I had to be.
    I return to who I already am.

2. Vulnerability

Reflection:

- When have I recently let myself be seen, and how did it feel?
- What beliefs am I holding about vulnerability that I'm ready to soften?

Affirmation:

My vulnerability is a strength.
I honor it as a doorway to connection, not a risk to be feared.

3. Trust

Reflection:

- Who or what helps me feel safe?
- Where can I practice trusting myself more deeply?

Affirmation:

I trust my inner knowing.
I trust the timing of my growth.
I trust myself to begin again.

4. Discernment

Reflection:

- How does my body speak when something is or isn't aligned?
- Where am I being called to protect my energy with love?

Affirmation:

I honor my yes.
I honor my no.
My discernment is sacred, and I trust it.

Reframing Old Beliefs

If you notice old programming surfacing—
like "I can't trust people," or "If I'm vulnerable, I'll be judged"—
see if you can gently reframe it.
You don't need to bypass the pain;
you only need to remind yourself of what's also true.

Here are a few examples:

Old belief: *"I need to protect myself at all costs."*
New truth: *"I am safe to be seen. I protect myself with love, not fear."*

Old belief: *"If I trust, I'll be hurt."*
New truth: *"I trust myself to choose wisely and heal fully, no matter what happens."*

You don't need to answer everything at once.
You don't need to force healing into a timeline.

Just keep returning.
Keep listening.
Keep choosing love over fear,
truth over performance,
and self-trust over self-abandonment.

You are already on your way.

Qualities of a Safe Person

When we talk about safety,
we're not just talking about physical safety.
We're talking about emotional, spiritual,
energetic, and relational safety.

Safe people help you feel seen,
respected, and at ease.
They don't demand you be impeccable.
They honor your truth
and invite you to stay connected to it.

These are the kind of people
we want to draw close—
and the kind of people
we can also learn to become.

Below are some of the qualities
that demonstrate what it means to be safe,
both in your relationships with others
and in your relationship with yourself.

Integrity
They do what they say they'll do.
Their values and behavior align.
They tell the truth, even when it's hard,
and they expect the same of others.

Trustworthiness
They follow through.
They don't disappear when things are inconvenient.
You know where you stand with them.

Empathy and Compassion
They listen without rushing to fix.
They try to understand your experience, not override it.
They offer care instead of control.

Emotional Regulation
They take responsibility for their emotions.
They can stay grounded in hard conversations.
They don't make you feel responsible for their reactions.

Accountability
They own their mistakes.
They repair harm.
They know their patterns and are doing the work to shift them.
They take responsibility for their actions *and* their healing.

Transparency
They communicate openly.
They don't play games or keep you guessing.
They let you in without creating confusion.

Respect for Boundaries
They don't test your limits.
They honor your no.
They respect your space to be your full self.

Support System

They have people and practices that keep them grounded.

They don't rely on you to be their everything.

They encourage healthy interdependence, not enmeshment.

Self-Awareness

They reflect often and meet themselves with honesty and compassion.

They practice self-love as a consistent way of being.

They tend to their own healing so others don't have to carry the weight.

Humility

They don't need to be right to feel okay.

They can learn, adjust, and own where they've missed the mark.

They value growth over ego.

We cultivate safety by showing up with consistency, honesty, and care.

We repair the damage when we get things wrong.

We create space for others to be themselves, without judgment or pressure.

And we extend that same grace to ourselves.

Becoming a Safe Place for Yourself and Others

Emotional safety isn't just something we receive.
It's something we create
for ourselves and for the people we love and choose.

As you begin to notice the qualities that make someone else feel safe,
it's just as important to turn that awareness inward.

Becoming a safe person doesn't mean never making mistakes.
It means being intentional.
It means knowing yourself deeply enough
to create safety from the inside out.

The more we do this,
the more we become the very kind of presence we long for.

Invitation

Before moving forward, pause.
Let yourself land.
Put your hand on your heart.
Take a deep breath in.
Feel your body, your truth, your presence, your heartbeat.
Let your shoulders soften.
Maybe light a candle. Sip something nourishing.
Create a moment of safety just for you.

This isn't a checklist. It's a return,
a way to meet yourself where you are with tenderness and intention.
You don't have to rush this work.
You just have to show up.

Reflection Prompts

Let these questions be a doorway inward.
You can explore them through journaling, quiet thought, movement, or conversation with someone safe.

- Am I open to vulnerability and authenticity?
- Do I honor the vulnerability of others?
- How do I respond when someone shares something tender or difficult with me? Do I offer presence, or do I try to fix or retreat?
- Am I emotionally available when it matters most?
- Do I take ownership of my actions and repair when needed?
- Am I consistent in my words and behavior, building trust over time?
- Do I respect others' boundaries and honor my own?
- Do I act in alignment with my values, even when it's inconvenient?
- Can I regulate my nervous system in conflict or stress? (And when I can't, do I notice it and return with grace?)
- Do I have a support system that helps me stay grounded and whole?
- And perhaps most importantly, do I practice self-love consistently and sincerely? Have I met myself, and am I committed to continuing that relationship?

Next Steps

You don't need to do it all.
Start small.
Pick one intention to carry with you:

- Speak one honest truth.
- Rest instead of exerting.
- Say no when you mean no.
- Let someone safe see the real you.
- Begin building trust with yourself, moment by moment.
- Revisit a boundary and adjust it with love.

You can also take time to identify one or two "safe people" in your life and reflect on what makes them feel that way.
Ask yourself, *How can I offer myself that same presence?*

Integration

Becoming wholehearted and wise isn't a destination,
but a journey: honest, soft, grounded, real.
It's a practice of showing up as you are, again and again.

Let this chapter be your compass and your ship,
guiding you through the four pillars of self-honoring,
carried by the grace of your resilience.

You are safe to be seen.
You are safe to be you.
You are already enough.
You can return to this knowing, over and over,
with love,
with intention,
with grace.

CHAPTER 10

Becoming My True Self

"The privilege of a lifetime is to become who you truly are."
—Carl Jung

Where We've Been, Where We're Going

In Chapter 9,
we explored the courageous path of choosing yourself,
not as a one-time act,
but as a daily devotion.

We named authenticity, vulnerability, trust, and discernment
as four foundational pillars
that act as a compass,
guiding you back to what is real.

We honored that healing isn't always loud.
Sometimes, it's steady,
gentle,
a quiet choosing of yourself
in the smallest of ways.

We circled back to graceful resilience
as the vessel that carries you.

It's a soft strength,
a rooted steadiness,
the kind that bends without breaking.

As you unlearn the roles that once defined you,
you begin to make space
for something deeper to rise:
the truth of who you are.

Now, in this chapter,
we step into that becoming.

We explore what it means
to live from the inside out:
to lead, love, and create from wholeness.

You don't need to become someone new.
You only need to remember
who you've always been—
and let that true self
finally take the lead.

My Journey Back to Myself

For over sixteen years, I built a business I was proud of:
a private therapy practice that offered safety, insight, and healing
to hundreds of souls.

It allowed me to serve others
while being fully present for my daughters
during their most formative years.

In many ways,
it helped me make sense of my own life.
If something good could come
from the chaos of my childhood
and the pain of early adulthood,
then maybe all of it had meaning.

I wanted to use what I had learned—
both as a self-healer and as a therapist—
to help others find their way through.
I wanted to offer what I never had:
a steady presence,
a listening ear,
a sense that they weren't alone.

For a long time, that was enough.

My world was full
with motherhood, caregiving, and meaning.

But something began to stir:
a quiet restlessness,
a deeper truth rising up from within.

The first whispers came years earlier.
In 2017, I began to consider coaching,
wondering if it might offer more freedom,
more creativity,
more of *me*.
But it wasn't time,
not yet.

Still, the questions stayed with me.
The creative discontent slowly caught fire.

By 2019,
I could feel the edges of my old shape fraying.
By 2023,
the truth became undeniable:

My office,
the space where I had held so much for others,
no longer held *me*.

One day, sitting in it alone,
I realized it felt like a structure that had once saved me
but that now contained me.

It was like a well-built room
with no windows.

I had outgrown the structure,
the licensing board,
the clinical forms.
The systems that once made me feel legitimate
now made me feel confined.

And then the deeper truth hit me:
I had chosen a career where my worth was measured
by how useful I was.

In this space, being "the helper" was assumed.
I could focus on others
while my voice, my needs, and my feelings
stayed in the background—
just like they did when I was growing up.

My career had become
a continuation of the very patterns I had spent decades healing from.

That realization shook me.

I had always been the keeper of secrets.
From childhood, I learned to carry what couldn't be spoken,
to absorb the tension in the room,
to hold space for others while silencing myself.

I became skilled at maintaining appearances,
making sure everything looked okay on the outside,
even when I was unraveling within.

It's no surprise I became a therapist.

My gifts for attunement,
deep listening,
and holding space without judgment
had served me well.

I still love the work.
I am honored by it.

But I evolved.
So I needed something different.

Alongside that realization came another one:
I was no longer in harmony
with the medical model of mental health.

I didn't believe in pathologizing pain.
I didn't want to reduce someone's lived experience
to a set of symptoms in a diagnostic box.

From the very beginning,
I had seen my clients as the experts of their own lives.

My role wasn't to fix or advise.
It was to walk beside them,
to reflect their wisdom back to them,
to hold space for what they already knew deep down.

That was still what I wanted,
but as I grew, I also wanted to bring more of *me* into the room.

I couldn't be just the clinician or healer anymore;
I needed to be the whole human.

Only then could I bring lived experience,
spiritual insight,
and a deep respect for healing that includes
the body, the energy field, and the soul into my practice.

My view had expanded.
And it was time for my life to expand with it.

Part of that shift came from my own healing.

I've always believed
I could not guide someone to a place
I wasn't willing to go to myself.

I've never wanted to ask anyone to do something
I wasn't willing to do.

The more I healed—
the more I listened to my body,
trusted my inner knowing,
and honored my truth—
the more places I could go,
and the more good I could do.

With healing, the truth became clearer:
It was time to walk a new path.

The journey would be for those I serve,
but also for me.

The Voice That Never Left

As a little girl, I filled notebooks with poems.
In graduate school, I felt the first real pull to write a book.
But life was full enough, so that dream was quietly placed on a shelf.

Still, it never left me.

The desire to create, to express, to share from my soul
was always there, waiting.

It's only in the last few years that I've begun to say yes
in a series of quiet, courageous steps.

And I'm still in process,
still learning,
still letting it all unfold.

I'm not here with a five-step plan or a perfect formula.
I'm here with open arms and an honest heart.

I'm beginning to walk as a coach, a mentor, a guide, a writer, a poet,
and a healer,
but even those words are evolving.

This work is becoming something new.
And so am I.

Turning Points and Soul Nudges

Some changes come in waves.
Others arrive like quiet invitations,
just enough to wake something inside you
you didn't realize was asleep.

In 2024, I joined a three-month coaching program
facilitated by Matt Hersh and Chet Morjaria,
two leaders who brought both strategy and soul to the process.

Matt had a way of asking the kind of questions
that bypassed surface answers
and went straight to the heart.

His presence was steady, warm, and deeply attuned,
never pushing but always inviting something deeper.

He would listen,
then gently ask things like,
"What would it feel like to trust that?"
or
"What if this dream is already unfolding, just more slowly than you
expected?"

He didn't tell me what to do.
Instead, he helped me hear myself more clearly.

And in that space,
something began to shift.
My vision expanded.

I started to believe in it, without having to be convinced,
simply because I felt it in my body:
possible, real, already becoming.

One day, in a group session,
Matt casually shared about his first reiki experience,
how it moved something in him
he hadn't known was stuck.

I had been curious about reiki for a while,
but that simple share was the spark I needed.
I scheduled a session at Blue Ridge Reiki that same week.

And it changed everything.

The moment the practitioner's hands hovered over my body,
I felt an ancient stillness,
a knowing I couldn't explain.
My body softened.
My mind quieted.
Tears welled, not from pain,
but from a deep sense of homecoming.

Something opened,
subtle but unmistakable.

It was like I had touched something sacred
I didn't even know I had been searching for.

These experiences weren't the end of the story.
But they helped me begin a new chapter
with more clarity, more courage, and more trust.

They reminded me that healing could be sacred,
that I didn't have to walk alone,
and that I could trust where I was being led.

Expanding Support

In early 2025, I traveled to the jungle of Mexico
to attend ACE Interstellar,
a spiritual entrepreneur retreat created by Mikey Sheridan and ACE
High Retreats.

It was my first international trip in over twenty years
and my first personal journey in nearly eight.
That leap felt both massive and right on time.

For a long time, I had poured everything into others.
Adventure, fun, and ease had fallen into the background.

Somewhere along the way,
I stopped believing I deserve good things—
or maybe I never fully knew it to begin with.

This retreat reminded me that I do,
that I always have,
and that there is more.

But the transformation didn't begin in the jungle.
It started long before I crossed the border.

I had already begun collecting evidence—
tiny signs of provision,
quiet moments of grace,
unexplainable synchronicities—
that reminded me I was never truly alone.

For so long, I believed it was all on me
to hold it all,
to fix it all,
to figure it all out.

But the more I softened,
the more I noticed
support was everywhere.

It was in my daughters:
in their love,
in their reflection of who I had been
and who I was becoming.

It was in nature:
in waterfalls that roared,
in rivers carving new paths without force,
in mountains standing rooted and unshaken,
in the way awe struck me
at every tree, every sunset, every bloom,
reminding me what it meant to feel alive.

It was in music:
in lyrics that arrived at just the right time,
in melodies that lifted something inside me.

It was in connections with people online:
their stories, their encouragement,
their honest reflections that made me feel less alone.

It was in the hat I bought from Matt Gottesman,
entrepreneur, writer, and creative force,
that simply read, *Nah, bigger. —God.*

That hat felt like a message,
a divine reminder that I didn't have to shrink,
that I could say yes to more.

By the time I arrived in the jungle,
my heart was already opening.

I met more of my soul family,
people who saw me,
held me,
reflected back a version of me
I hadn't fully embraced yet.

I had more deep, authentic conversations in a few days
than I'd had in years.

We danced.
We laughed.
We stretched.
We healed.

The retreat magnified what had already begun.

Something came alive in me again:
something wild,
awake,
and untamed.

Ironically, I left the jungle changed
because I'd remembered what I never had:

I can trust joy.
I can trust connection.
I can trust myself.

More Me Than I've Ever Been

In this season of my life,
I've begun to see myself with new eyes.

I no longer look through a lens of brokenness,
but through an understanding
that brings compassion,
clarity,
and curiosity.

I've always felt deeply,
noticed everything,
and carried far more than I let on.

I thought that was just how I moved through the world.
But I've started to understand it in a fuller context.

I'm a 5/1 Manifesting Generator in Human Design,
an INFJ in the Myers-Briggs Type Indicator,
and an Enneagram 2 with strong 4 energy.

Each framework I studied gave me language for things I had always
sensed:
my drive to help,
my need for depth and integrity,
my longing to be seen beyond what I give,
and the pressure I've carried
to perform, to please, and to hold it all together.

I took the Myers-Briggs test in college
and was typed as an ISTJ:
logical, practical, rule-following, and task-oriented.

At the time,
that made sense.
I had buried my emotions.
I trusted facts over intuition.
I coped by controlling what I could.

Years later, I took the test again
and came back as an INFJ:
intuitive, deeply feeling, empathetic,
driven by meaning and inner vision.

That shift told me everything.

It reflected the journey I'd been on:
from self-protection to self-permission,
from suppression to truth,
from acting as who I thought I needed to be
to returning to who I actually am.

More recently,
I've begun exploring the different ways neurodivergence,
both innate and acquired, has touched my story.
Instead of seeing pathology, I've noticed patterns.

When I look at both of my parents,
the environments I adapted to,
and the ways I've masked, coped, and observed deeply,
I see it all more clearly.

I don't need a diagnosis,
just like I never needed a label for cPTSD
to recognize the shape of trauma in my body.

What I need,
what I've always needed,
is permission to be exactly who I am:

fully,
tenderly,
and without explanation.

I'm not claiming a fixed identity.
I'm living a deepening one.

More being.
Less explaining.

And it feels expansive,
liberating,
right on time.

I've never felt more like myself,
and I wouldn't trade that for anything.

I Will Not Abandon Myself Again

I've always connected well with people.
I'm warm,
friendly,
and open-hearted.

But underneath that,
I've often been a loner,
a quiet processor,
an observer,
a deeply private soul.

I learned early on
that my needs didn't matter,
that my voice was too much,
that my feelings were too big.

I knew how to play small
and how to keep a good front.

But that's not who I am.

Choosing to see myself,
to hear myself,
and to love and honor myself
has taken monumental courage.

And I'm not going back.

Those earlier versions of me
worked hard to survive.
I thank them.

But I'm not living in a box anymore.
I'm not shrinking
to make anyone else comfortable.

I will never abandon myself again.

A Quiet Miracle

We all read through the lenses of our own experiences,
our own biases,
our own illusions.

And I can't control what people take away from this book.
But what I *can* do is be clear.

I was painfully shy,
socially awkward,
anxious around people.
I mostly preferred being alone.

So to be where I am now—
still a little quirky
but at ease in my own skin,
comfortable around others,
and able to connect without losing myself—
is a miracle.

Here I am:
not playing small,
not hiding,
using my voice,
knowing I am supported.

This life I live
is the result of *graceful resilience*
put into practice.

I love myself—all of me.
I know myself.
And I am living my best life.

That, to me,
is everything.

What Embodiment Really Means

Embodiment is not a practice of faking authenticity,
that is, looking like you have it all together.
It's not a curated version of the truth.

Embodiment means *living* what you know.
It's when your values show up in your voice,
in your choices,
and in the way you move through the world,
especially when no one is watching.

It's listening to your body,
not just your thoughts.
It's honoring what you feel,
even when it's messy.
It's trusting your intuition,
even when the path ahead is unclear.

Embodiment is less about getting it right
and more about staying real.
You don't have to be perfect.
You just have to be honest,
especially with yourself.

Every Part Belongs

Wholeness isn't the achievement of an idealized version of yourself.
It's the practice of making space for all of you:
your strength and your struggle,
your confidence and your doubt,
your clarity and your questions.

It's not born of control,
but of acceptance.

It's standing in your own life and saying,
All of me is welcome here.

Living with integrity begins with self-trust.
The more you trust your body,
your timing,
your yes,
and your no,
the more your life reflects who you really are.

Self-trust doesn't mean you never wobble.
It means when you do,
you know how to come back.

Where are your feet?
Stay there,
in the moment.

But what about when you're not sure
if it's intuition...or anxiety?

That's something I've wrestled with
and that I hear from clients all the time.

It's like when you want to leave a party
where you don't know anyone,
and you feel that tightening in your chest:
Is this my intuition saying "this isn't my space,"
or is it anxiety trying to protect me from discomfort?

Anxiety is loud, urgent, and grasping.
It speaks in fear and what-ifs.

Intuition is quieter,
more steady.
It doesn't panic; it nudges.

Anxiety wants control.
Intuition trusts what's true.

Anxiety tightens your chest.
Intuition gives you room to breathe.

It's not always easy to tell the difference,
especially when your nervous system is on high alert
or your past is echoing in the background.

But the more you slow down
and notice what's happening inside,
the easier it becomes to tell which voice is speaking.

And yes,
even anxiety is welcome here.

It shouldn't get to take the wheel,
but it does deserve credit for trying to keep you safe.

You can greet it with compassion
without giving it control.
You can listen
without letting it shape your choices.
You can understand
what it's trying to tell you that you need.

Wholeness means every part has a place,
but not every part leads.

And when all parts speak—
not just your mind,
but your body, your emotions, your spirit, and your energy—
listen.

Your mind may hold old stories.
Your body carries memory and quiet wisdom.
Your emotions speak truth.
Your spirit holds purpose and connection.
Your energy sets boundaries and reveals resonance.

When one part speaks, listen.
When all parts speak together,
trust what they're saying.

As Nietzsche wrote,
"There is more wisdom in your body than in your deepest
philosophy."

This is the wisdom we come home to.
You don't need to chase it;
simply notice it:
in stillness,
in sensation,
in the quiet clarity that rises
when all of you is invited to the table.

Letting the Tears Come

Crying is one of the most natural forms of regulation we have.
It's not a sign of weakness;
it's a release valve.

Tears are how the body moves emotional energy.
They calm the nervous system,
restore balance,
and help us return to a grounded state.

After crying, our breath deepens.
Our muscles soften.
Our heartbeat slows.

Crying doesn't automatically mean something's wrong.
It often means something is being released:
a wave of feeling,
a long-held ache,
a truth that's ready to be witnessed.

You don't need to hide your tears.
You can let them speak
what words can't carry.

Sometimes, crying *is* the healing.

When the tears come—
or even when they don't,
but you feel something rising—
pause and ask:

Is this fear...or truth?
Is my body bracing or softening?

Then trust the answer.

Where It Really Lives

You don't need a retreat
or a breakthrough moment
to live in alignment with who you are.

It shows up in the everyday:
in how you start your morning,
how you nourish yourself,
how you speak to yourself
when things don't go as planned,
how you say no (even when it's hard),
how you move through your day
with presence instead of pressure.

Living your truth means
your actions, your words, and your energy
reflect your deepest values.

It looks like
honoring your needs with boundaries,
asking for help when you need it,
trusting your emotions as guidance,
listening to your body's quiet wisdom,
and speaking your truth,
even when it feels vulnerable.

When all parts of you are allowed to coexist
without shame,
without rejection,
and without force,
you begin to feel like yourself again.

When your life begins to reflect your truth,
you don't just talk about what matters;
you *live* it.

And that's where aliveness begins.

You need not strive,
only know.

You need not fix,
only accept yourself
fully,
as you are,
right here.

Affirmations for the Journey

I trust myself to return.
I allow all parts of me to belong.
I move through life at my own pace.
I am safe to be fully me.
My truth is not too much; it's just right.
I don't need to earn rest, softness, or support.
I am already becoming.

This Is How You Begin Again

As you move through these practices, remember:
Embodiment is not a destination.
It's a practice,
a yes to you.

Some days it will feel effortless.
Other days, it may feel tender, uncertain, or hard.

Keep showing up.

But also know
it's okay to pause.
It's okay to rest.

Slowing down doesn't mean you're doing it wrong.
It means you're listening.

Trust yourself:
your body,
your intuition,
your emotions.

They are not obstacles.
They are messengers
guiding you back to your most authentic self.

Every small step matters.
Each boundary honored,
each truth spoken,

each breath that returns you to now
is part of the becoming.

And when you slip (because you will),
meet yourself with compassion.

You're not starting over.
You're remembering.
Repair is part of the practice, too.

When someone crosses a boundary,
you get to choose again.
You get to speak, to clarify,
to stand in your truth
with love and steadiness.

You get to return,
again and again,
to yourself.

Where You Can Exhale

The spaces we inhabit
physically, relationally, and energetically
can either nourish our healing
or quietly drain us.

Ask yourself gently,
Does my home feel like a refuge?
Do my relationships invite ease and honesty?
Do I have places where I can fully exhale?

Creating a sanctuary isn't about getting everything "right."
Don't worry about having perfect furniture,
ideal schedules,
or a decluttered life.

What matters is intention.

Choose what supports your nervous system,
what lets you soften,
what lets you breathe.

Surround yourself with quiet
when you need quiet,
color
when you crave beauty,
and movement
when your body longs to release.

Sanctuary is found in moments
when you're not performing,

in spaces where your tears are welcome
and nothing needs to be fixed.

It's in the walk
where your thoughts slow
and your breath deepens.

It's in the conversation
where your soul feels safe to speak.

It's in the corner of your room
that allows you to exhale,
in the playlist
that reconnects you to your strength.

Creating sanctuary is a way of saying,
I matter.
My peace matters.
All of me is worth honoring.

Let your environment reflect
what you now believe about yourself:

You are worthy of care.
You are allowed to feel safe.
You deserve to feel at home
inside your own life.

Invitation

This isn't a chapter you finish,
but a practice you return to.
It's a way of showing up,
of choosing yourself, again and again,
in quiet moments,
in messy moments,
in the daily rhythm of being human and becoming whole.

You don't need a major life shift to be your true self.
You just need presence,
curiosity,
and will.

Find a comfortable space, inside or out.
Let your breath settle.
Let your body speak.
Let these reflections guide you inward.

Reflection Prompts

- What does "embodiment" mean to me right now?
- Where in my life am I already living in alignment with my values?
- Where am I still holding back, and why?
- What would it feel like to honor my emotions, even the uncomfortable ones?
- What spaces or relationships feel like sanctuary?
- What is one small change I could make today that would bring me closer to myself?

Next Steps

- Begin your day with presence: place your hand on your heart, take three slow breaths, and ask, "What do I need today?"
- Move your body intuitively: stretch, dance, walk, sway. Let your body lead, not your to-do list.
- Speak your truth in a safe space, even if your voice shakes. One honest sentence is enough to begin.
- Create simple rituals: a morning grounding, an evening exhale, a song you play when you need to come home to yourself.
- Name a need—emotional, physical, or spiritual—and meet it with kindness instead of judgment.
- Practice noticing: When do you feel most like yourself? Where are you? What are you doing? Who are you with?
- Set a gentle boundary or make a choice that honors your energy. It doesn't have to be dramatic to be powerful.
- Return to your sanctuary, whether it's a room, a walk, a playlist, a memory, or your breath. Let it remind you that you are safe.
- Ask, *What would it look like to live this truth today?* Let one small action move you forward.

What I Hope You Remember

You don't need to have it all figured out.
You don't need a perfect plan or a flawless path.

You just need presence,
honesty,
and the courage to keep choosing yourself.

I hope you remember these truths:
You can be strong and soft at the same time.
You can be whole and still healing.
You can hold space for your pain
without letting it define you.
You can start over, again and again, and it still counts.

You don't have to arrive anywhere.
You get to live each day as it comes.
You get to grow at your own pace.
You get to be honest without having to be perfect.

You are already enough.
You are already worthy.
You are already becoming who you were always meant to be.

Integration

Take a breath.
Let it settle.
Let these truths move beyond the page
and into your body,
into your choices,
into your presence.

You don't have to get it all right.
You just have to keep coming home to yourself.

Embodiment asks for honesty, not perfection.
Presence, not performance.
Gentleness, not judgment.

And always trust.
Trust in your own unfolding.
Trust in what is blessed and unseen.
Trust that God (or whatever name you give to the sacred)
meets you in every step of your return.

You are not doing this alone.
You are guided,
held,
loved.

This journey isn't separate from your spirit;
it is the very place where your humanity and divinity meet.

With every return,
you are deepening into who you already are.

Let this chapter be a gentle touchstone,
a light you can return to again and again
to remember what it feels like
to be whole,
to be guided,
to be home.

CHAPTER 11

Thriving with Grace

*"You do not have to be good. You do not have to walk on your knees
for a hundred miles through the desert, repenting."*
—Mary Oliver

Where We've Been, Where We're Going

In Chapter 10, we explored the courage it takes to live as yourself,
to trust your timing,
speak your truth,
and walk your own path.

We let go of roles that no longer fit,
and we reclaimed parts of ourselves that were waiting to be seen.

And we remembered that
authenticity is not a goal;
it's a way of being.

Now, in this final chapter,
we begin to explore what it means to thrive.

Thriving is more than surviving.
It's living with intention,
from a place of wholeness.

You don't need to chase more;
you just need to embrace what matters most.

This chapter is an invitation
to create space,
to breathe deeply,
and to live with passion and purpose.

Let your life expand
through mindfulness,
trust,
and grace.

Thriving Isn't a Destination

What does it really mean to thrive?
It's more than healing
and surviving.

It's living
fully,
unapologetically,
and expansively.

Survival taught you how to endure,
how to stay safe,
how to keep going.

Thriving invites something else entirely.
It calls you to open,
to receive,
to create,
to allow grace to support you, especially when strength alone is not
enough.

It doesn't mean you'll never stumble, doubt, or start over.
It means you move in rhythm
between surrender and action,
rest and movement,
grace and growth.

Thriving isn't concerned with arriving.
It's staying rooted in what matters:
living your truth,
one choice at a time.

It's not gripping the edge or running on empty.
It's having space to breathe,
to be,
to give,
to receive.

It's living from your wholeness,
from a grounded trust in your worth
and the grace that's carried you here.

Thriving, for me, also means staying awake to wonder,
being moved by the way rivers keep running,
flowers dare to bloom,
and sunsets turn the sky into prayer.

It's remembering how to play,
how to dance barefoot under the stars,
how to laugh until my body feels lighter,
how to chase beauty
just because it makes me feel alive.

Healing gave me back my wonder.
Loving myself gave me back my joy.

Thriving is letting life be the miracle it is—
and letting that miracle move you, every day.

It's stepping into your future self
and honoring the ones who got you here:

- the inner child, who survived with tenderness and instinct;
- the inner teen, who longed for freedom in silence;
- the shadow self, who held your pain until it could be seen.

Thriving is loving all of them back into the light.
This isn't the end of your story;
it's the beginning of how you live it.

To thrive is to

- live without shrinking or silencing yourself.
- treat your needs, boundaries, and desires as sacred.
- embrace the full spectrum of who you are:
  your joy and your grief,
  your strength and your softness.
- create a life of meaning, connection, and expansion.
- trust your rhythm, your voice, and your worth.

Thriving doesn't mean bypassing pain.
It means moving through life with presence and courage,
with self-trust
and the unwavering belief
that your life belongs to you.

When you build spaces that calm your nervous system,
foster relationships that nourish your spirit,
and stop outsourcing your value,
you begin to come alive.

And that belief
that you are allowed to live this way
starts now.

The Grace Within Thriving

Grace isn't loud.
She doesn't push.
She doesn't demand.
She meets you
gently
in the pause between breaths,
in the softness after the storm.

She is the hand on your back
when you're tired of holding it all,
the still voice that says,
You don't have to earn this life.
You get to live it.

Grace walks beside you
when strength says to press on
and your soul says to rest.

She's in the moments you forgive yourself,
in the days you choose peace over striving,
and in the breath that reminds you
you're already enough.

Grace is how we thrive:
by remembering
we are already held.

I Chose Myself

In a virtual session with my intuitive guide, Devon,
she shared something with me afterward.

She'd often share insights and impressions,
things she noticed or heard during each session.

This time, she described the presence of a male energy,
someone whose essence had come through.

That might sound strange,
but in intuitive or energy work,
we sometimes connect with emotions, memories,
or even the energetic imprint of loved ones,
especially those who have passed on
but who still remain close in unseen ways.

I didn't know who it was at first.
But when she described
his spirit and his energy,
it hit me.

It was my brother.

His words were simple but powerful:
"Proud of you, kid.
You've been through a lot,
but you make it look easy."

Talk about feeling seen.
Talk about feeling supported.

He was right:
I have been through a lot,
and no one came to save me.

Because no one was supposed to.

That realization stirred something deep inside me.

There was no external savior.
There never had been.

I have always been my own anchor.
I have always been enough.

My healing didn't begin the moment I was validated by others.
It began the moment I chose myself.

It didn't happen only once,
but again and again,
in the quiet, hard, unseen moments.

That is self-worth.
That is self-love.
That is authenticity.

Am I delusional?
Absolutely—
in the best way.

I embrace all possibilities for myself,
and I want the same for you.

And just beyond where I stand now,
I see her:
my future self.

She is waiting for me,
happy and radiating.

She calls me forward,
cheering me on:

"You've got this.
Look where we are.
Look at the life we created!"

She already knows.
She sees it.
She feels it.
She's already living it.

Now, I'm catching up to her.

I have transmuted my pain into massive purpose.
This journey has lasted decades.

And I have been relentless in my healing,
tenacious in my growth.

I wanted this life.
So I fought for it.

And I will protect what I've created,
by the grace and strength of God.

I can't stop.
I won't stop.

The Holy Pause

And still,
among my thriving,
life brought me to my knees again.

Ten days after my mom died,
I was in the ER with a kidney stone,
feeling a wave of pain I didn't see coming.

I waited for surgery,
feeling weak and worn out.

Two days later,
as directed by the doctor,
I pulled the stent out myself...

and ended up back in the ER
in excruciating pain...

only to be sent home
with pain meds
and told to follow up.

I did.
And I'm grateful I did,
because I was finally given antibiotics.

I had seven days of relief,
seven days of validation,
even if my doctor refused to name it for what it was:
a kidney infection.

I had stood up for myself
and finally received the help I needed.

My friends, all functional practitioners,
read the labs and confirmed what I already felt:

the inflammation,
the high neutrophils,
the quiet war my body was fighting
while I was still grieving
and trying to hold everything together.

I had to come to a full stop,
to lie down,
to feel it all:

the loss,
the grief,
the pain.

I had to embrace the unknown.

And I know,
even with all this pain,
that good is coming in.

In this space in between,
in the pause where what *was* no longer fits
and what's *next* is still forming,

I'm learning to breathe again.

This space is hard.
But it's holy.

My purpose and passion are still evolving.
All of me is.

What's meant for me will not miss me.

And this version of me?
I'm loving her more every day.

She trusts divine timing.
She moves with intention.
She doesn't force the next chapter,
but allows it.

She knows herself enough
to fight for what she knows she needs.

And she listens to her body enough
to grieve when she needs to grieve.

She is learning
how to thrive.

A Promise in Ink

In 2008, I got a tattoo on my wrist that reads,
"Breathe."

Even then, I knew it was symbolic, multilayered,
a reminder to slow down,
to stay present,
to live fully, even in the hard moments.

Over time, its meaning has only expanded.

Breath is more than a function;
it's a foundation.
It connects body to spirit.
It anchors us to the now.
It is the first thing we gain when we enter this world
and the last thing we release when we leave it.

That single word became a lifeline,
a return,
a quiet promise to keep choosing life,
one conscious, thriving breath at a time.

The Current Knows

Trust the whisper within,
the quiet nudge, the knowing.

Trust the hands unseen,
the breath that moves the tide.

Surrender.
Let the current carry you.
Let the weight fall.
Let the river shape the stone.

It is unfolding,
not a moment too soon,
not a second too late,
only ever right on time.

The Art of Living from Love

You are not broken.
You are whole,
because you dared to gather every piece of your life
and call it sacred.

You are not here just to heal.
You are here to love,
to create,
to become.

You are allowed to imagine
and build
and dream
and expand.

You are a creator.
Whether you realize it or not,
you are creating your life every single day:

through your choices,
through your boundaries,
through how you speak to yourself,
how you nourish your body,
how you offer love to your own reflection,
how you show up in your relationships,
how you move through your mornings.

Creation isn't reserved for artists.
It's for all of us.
It's in the way you rise,

the way you plate your food,
the way you choose stillness or song,
strength or softness,
truth or silence.

When you begin to create your life
from a place of love—
from self-love, from your values,
from your healing, from your joy—

you begin to live with purpose instead of pattern.
You stop unconsciously repeating what was
and start intentionally shaping what will be.

You start thriving.

That is creation.
That is love in motion.

You have surpassed surviving,
healing,
and even becoming.

You are now creating,
with every breath,
with every act of love.

Thriving Is Holistic

To truly thrive,
you don't just think your way forward.

You feel.
You rest.
You move.
You nourish.
You connect.

Thriving happens when you honor all of who you are:
the parts that are easy to understand or put into words,
but also the parts that move through sensation,
intuition,
creativity,
and trust.

Thriving transcends mindset;
it is integration across your whole being.

Ways to Restore and Realign

1. Mentally:
by challenging old beliefs,
quieting inner noise,
and speaking truth over yourself with compassion.

2. Emotionally:
by honoring your feelings,
allowing space for all of you,
and gently releasing what no longer serves you.

3. Physically:
by tending to your body's needs, that is,
resting when you're tired,
moving with care,
and nourishing yourself consistently.

4. Spiritually:
by staying connected to something greater
(God, nature, your higher self)
and remembering you're not alone,
even in uncertainty.

5. Creatively/Energetically:
by recognizing what drains your inspiration,
knowing what fuels your light,
and giving yourself permission to pause,
to play,
to dream again.

6. Relationally:
by choosing relationships that nourish you,
setting boundaries without guilt,
and seeking connection that uplifts rather than depletes.

7. Sensorially:
by creating moments of stillness,
stepping away from noise, screens, and overstimulation,
and letting your nervous system soften into calm.

Rest Is Part of It

Thriving doesn't require constant movement.
It isn't a never-ending climb.

It's knowing when to be still,
when to soften,
when to let yourself exhale.

Rest is not a reward
you earn after doing enough.

It's part of the rhythm
of living well.

There are many kinds of rest,
and we need all of them.

Types of Rest

1. Mental Rest:
Quiet the constant stream of thoughts.

2. Emotional Rest:
Let go of what you no longer need to carry.

3. Physical Rest:
Give your body space to heal.

4. Spiritual Rest:
Trust that you're held, even when you don't have answers.

5. Energetic/Creative Rest:
Step back so inspiration can return.

6. Relational Rest:
Choose connection that restores instead of depletes.

7. Sensory Rest:
Turn down the volume of the world around you.

Rest is a way to listen.
It's how you recalibrate,
how you return to your center,
how you make space
for the voice within you
to rise again.

You are not lazy for needing it.
You are not weak for pausing.
You are wise.

Rest does not take you off your path;
it's what helps you stay on it.

She Was Always Speaking

Food and movement have always been part of my life,
but not always from a place of freedom or love.

Growing up, food was about control.
It was monitored, withheld,
and sometimes used as leverage.

I had to ask for what I needed, though I rarely did,
because the message was clear:
Your needs are too much.

Scarcity wasn't just financial.
It lived in the air we breathed:
emotional, energetic, relational.

There was never a "just right,"
never full permission to exist as I was.

Thinness was overemphasized.
Even when I was a young mom,
my own mother gave me fat-burning pills—
even though I never weighed more than 105 pounds.

But over time,
I stopped living by anyone else's definition of wellness or worth.

I started listening to my body,
trusting her,
nourishing her,

honoring what she asked for
and avoiding what she rejected.

Letting go of the old programming didn't happen all at once.
It happened gradually
as I returned to myself.

So when I was diagnosed with both hyperparathyroidism and severe
osteoporosis,
even after doing everything "right,"
I was devastated.

I had been eating well, moving daily, practicing self-love,
and trusting in divine protection.

And still, something deeper was asking to be seen.

As I struggled to keep weight on after being diagnosed,
my mother didn't say anything to me.

But she told my daughter I looked "too thin."

It was another moment of being scrutinized without support,
another layer of sadness added to an already difficult time.

All this revealed buried beliefs:
that I wasn't supported,
that asking for help wasn't safe,
that my needs were a burden.

They invited me to look at how much I'd carried in silence,
how often I had silenced myself,

how often I had prioritized my mother's voice over my own,
how hard I had worked to stay strong.

Making these connections didn't erase the healing I had already
done;
it allowed a deeper level of healing to take place.

It gave me a more complete picture,
and with that, a more compassionate one.

I welcomed every version of me.
Each one survived with the wisdom she had.
Each one did the best she could.

Now, I choose differently.
I speak up.
I ask for what I need
and don't take on what I don't want.
I allow myself to be supported.
I am open to receive.

And I believe my body is responding.

My bones are rebuilding:
my most recent DEXA scan showed a significant increase in bone
density,
especially in my hips.

My muscles are growing.
My nervous system is softening.
I feel restoration happening at the cellular level.

Even my food sensitivities, while still present,
have become unexpected teachers.

They've invited me to speak up,
tune in,
and stop pretending
when my body is asking for care.

I used to feel uncomfortable asking for a menu change at a
restaurant.
I didn't want to be a bother.

Now, I ask with ease.
And sometimes, I even smile to myself.

My body has always been trying to get my attention.
And now, I'm listening.

My mother has passed now.
And her voice, once so loud in my head,
no longer takes up much space.
I bless her.
I release her.
And I live by the voice within me.

This is what healing looks like to me now:
far from rigid
and flawless,

it's intentional,
intuitive,
loving,
and real.

And I am so incredibly grateful.

That's why every day feels like a gift:
because now I know
I get to live this life.

I Get To

There's a shift that happens
when you begin to see your life through the lens of gratitude,
as much for the big moments
as for the quiet, ordinary ones.

I get to make my bed.
I get to do the laundry.
I get to care for my body.
I get to work.
I get to rest.
I get to create.
I get to pay bills.
I get to walk into a home with heat and air and running water.
I get to choose how I respond to what life brings me.

What once felt heavy
still feels hard sometimes,
but it no longer feels like a burden.
Because now I meet it with presence instead of pressure,
with love instead of fear.

Even the challenges carry wisdom.
Even the disruptions reveal what matters.

I've always been a grateful person,
seeing the glass half full, even when it hurt.
That perspective helped me endure.
It helped me survive.

Now, it helps me thrive.
I don't pretend things are always good;
I simply remember that life as a whole is a blessing.

I get to live this life.
And for that,
I am deeply, endlessly grateful.

Invitation

A Sacred Pause Before Your Next Chapter
Before you move on, I invite you to pause. Drop your shoulders.
Find a quiet, comfortable space: indoors, outdoors, wherever you feel most at ease.
Grab a drink. Open your journal or your laptop.
Let this be time just for you.

A Simple Breath Practice
Close your eyes if that feels safe.
Place one hand on your heart and one on your belly.
Begin to notice your breath, without trying to change it.
Let it move in and out naturally.

If it feels supportive, try this rhythm:
- Inhale slowly through your nose for a count of four.
- Hold for a count of two.
- Exhale gently through your mouth for a count of six.

Repeat for three to five rounds, or adjust in any way that feels good to your body.
There's no right way to do this.
The goal isn't control; it's presence.

Let your breath settle you.
Let it bring you into your body.
Let it remind you, *You're here, and that matters.*

Reflection Prompts

Set Your Intention
Now that you've settled into your body, take a quiet moment
to ask yourself,

What do I most need right now? What am I ready to receive?

You don't need to overthink it.
Let your intention rise from a place of clarity.
Hold it gently as you move through the reflection questions,
one breath, one truth, one moment at a time.

These prompts are here to support, not to pressure.
You don't have to answer them all, and you don't have to rush.
Let them meet you where you are.
Be curious, gentle, and open. That's more than enough.

- What does thriving truly look and feel like for me in this season of life?
- What would it look like to live from grace instead of grind?
- Where in my life is grace asking me to soften? Where might trust or surrender offer me more peace?
- Where in my life am I being invited to trust the unfolding, even when the outcome is unclear?
- What story has my body been trying to tell me? What would it look like to listen now with trust instead of fear?
- Where in my life have I struggled to ask for what I need? What's shifted? What's still asking for a voice?
- What commitments, big or small, am I ready to make to honor the next version of myself?
- What am I ready to release so I can step more fully into my power and truth?
- If my future self were to look back at me today, what would they see? What would they whisper to me with love and clarity?
- If no one else is coming to save me and my transformation is truly in my hands, how does that feel? What does that free me to choose?
- Can I allow the possibility that I am already enough, just as I am, while still evolving?

Next Steps

Let this be a threshold moment,
a quiet crossing between who you were and who you're becoming.

Now, choose one small thing to carry forward.
You don't have to prove anything.
You don't have to perform.
Just take one honest step.

Here are some suggestions:
- Speak a truth you've been holding in.
- Create a daily pause to check in with your body.
- Choose grace when you feel the pull to hustle.
- Make one brave request for support.
- Do something just for the joy of it.

Whatever you choose,
let it be enough.
Let it root you more deeply in the knowing of your authentic self.

Integration

Take a breath.
Let yourself feel the fullness of how far you've come.

You've tended to the tender parts.
You've softened old stories.
You've chosen presence over perfection.
And you've dared to imagine a life that honors the truth of who you are.

This is not the end.
It's the beginning of how you live now:
with intention,
with curiosity,
with trust in your own becoming.

Let grace be your companion
in the stillness
and in the steps that follow.

You have made it past surviving.
Now you are creating,
expressing,
thriving.

You don't need to do it all at once.
You just need to keep showing up
as the person you no longer hide.

You are ready.
And life—
a real, beautiful, ordinary, sacred life—
is ready for you, too.

FINAL INVITATION

You've come so far,
but the journey doesn't end here.
You're allowed to keep going,
to keep expanding,
to keep choosing yourself,
to keep releasing what no longer serves you.

Pick one small step,
or simply rest in the knowing that you're already enough.

And if something in these pages has spoken to you,
if you feel a spark, an opening, a resonance,
I'd love to stay connected.
I'm also open to aligned collaborations, co-creations, and
conversations.

You can learn more about me, explore reflections, next steps, and
offerings at
www.theedgeofenough.info the heart of the book journey.
You can also visit www.energizewithanne.com for a fuller picture
of my work.

Or find me on Instagram, Facebook, and TikTok:
@energizewithanne
And LinkedIn: Anne Webb

You don't have to walk this path alone.
Go gently.
Let grace guide you.
Stay open.
Trust your unfolding.

Your story is still being written.
And it's yours now.

You were never too much.
You were always just enough.

ACKNOWLEDGMENTS

To God:
Thank You for Your unwavering presence,
boundless love, steady protection,
and gentle whispers that remind me, again and again,
I am never alone.
Your grace has held me, shaped me, and carried me
through every fire and rebirth.
I offer this book as a prayer, a song, a testament to Your love.

To my angels and guides,
seen and unseen, ancient and eternal:
Thank you for protecting, guiding, and loving me
through every twist, every ache, every awakening.
You remind me that I am always supported,
always surrounded by light.

To my daughter Mia:
Your unstoppable spirit, unshakable will,
and fearless heart call me to stand taller,
dream bigger, and walk boldly with unwavering conviction.
Your fire is not just strength; it's protection, passion, and the
relentless pursuit of truth.

To my daughter Zoe:
Your deep soul, quiet strength, and poetic heart reveal
beauty in the unseen.
You remind me that vulnerability is power.
Your presence is a refuge, your wisdom an anchor,
your love a language all its own.

From the beginning, we've been the "Can-Do Girls,"
meeting challenges with grit, heart, and an unshakable
belief in possibility.
You both remind me daily of the power of love,
the grace of becoming,
and the infinite potential of a hopeful heart.

To my sister Kris:
You were the first to light the torch of healing in our lineage.
Your journey showed me what was possible.
Thank you for your love, your belief in me,
and your unwavering support.
You've held space for my evolution in ways only a sister can.

To every client I've ever worked with:
Thank you for trusting me with your stories, your hearts,
and your healing.
You've allowed me to offer my love, my energy, my presence,
and my truth.
Your courage has shaped me.
I carry every session, every sacred moment,
with deep honor and gratitude.

To my support circle,
the friends who checked in, the healers who held space, the mentors
who believed in me,
the colleagues who reflected my gifts back to me,
and every person who offered a word of encouragement, a safe space,
or a reminder of what's possible:
Thank you.
Your steady presence and deep belief helped carry me forward when I
doubted myself.

To those whose impact has been especially deep,
Mikey, Zach, and the entire ACE family:
Thank you for showing me that soul family is real,
that people truly stand beside one another, and that I am worthy of
experiencing that kind of love.

To Rainier and The Creators Collective:
Thank you for holding a space where I could return to my creativity
with love, safety, and fire.
To the fellow Creators who walked beside me,
thank you for your presence and encouragement.

To Chet, Matt, and the Impact Accelerator group:
Thank you for offering me a space where I felt safe to be present,
to be seen and heard, and to begin the process of telling my story.

To Devon of Enlighten & Empower:
Thank you for helping me see the obvious
and seemingly small things
that have, in truth, altered the course of my life.
Thank you for facilitating expansion for more
and for reminding me that connection is real and I never walk alone.
You are part of my evidence.

To Nancee of Blue Ridge Reiki:
Thank you for your warmth, compassion, and intuitive presence.
You helped me receive deep healing and insights
and showed me my own capacity to help others
through energy healing.

To Jordan, my hairstylist and embodied beauty mirror:
Thank you for your gentle hands,
your open heart, and your sacred space that lets my soul feel seen.

To Ashley, my massage therapist:
Thank you for the safe, nurturing touch that has helped
my body feel like home again.

To those following and supporting me on social media:
Thank you for reading my words, witnessing my evolution,
and reflecting love back to me.
Your genuine interest and presence matter more than you know.
Your encouragement has helped me stay the course,
keep sharing, and keep believing.

To the poets, writers, singers, and creators of every kind
who dare to share their truth out loud:
Thank you for showing me this dream is possible.
Your courage lights the way.

To my readers:
You are why this story needed to be told.
May you feel yourself reflected in these pages.
May you remember that resilience is your birthright
and that love—true, wild, courageous love—is always possible.
Even on the edge of enough,
you are already whole.

To everyone who crosses paths with this book:
Thank you for witnessing my journey and for opening
your heart to these words.

To all who have shaped me, whether in a single
moment or over several years:
Thank you for helping me become who I am.

To those I have yet to meet:
I look forward with eager excitement and a heart full of love.
I believe in all possibilities,
and I believe we are already connected in ways we cannot yet see.

And to Mia and Zoe again:
Thank you for the love, the lessons, and the grace.
You are my heart's greatest treasures.
Together, we are unstoppable.
And together, with every heart that dares to hope, heal, and rise,
we can change this world.

APPENDIX

From Survival Roles to True Self

Identity	Core Longing	Small Question	Way of Coping	What They Lost	What They Gained	The Mistaken Gain
The Driven Doer	To feel worthy beyond what they achieve	Who am I if I'm not achieving?	Striving, overachieving, pushing through	Rest, ease, internal permission to slow down	Praise, success, external validation	Sense of purpose through productivity
The Sensitive Soul	To be cared for as deeply as they care for others	What if honoring my needs is the most loving thing I can do?	Attuning to others, absorbing emotional energy	Their own needs, energy, and nervous system regulation	Trust from others, a sense of emotional purpose	Safety through caretaking
The Heart-Centered Harmonizer	To be accepted without self-abandonment	What if honoring my truth is the only way to feel truly connected?	People-pleasing, avoiding conflict, suppressing needs	Their voice, preferences, and sense of sovereignty	Relational safety, temporary connection	Approval through self-silencing
The Lost Child	To be seen and known without fear	What if being seen doesn't threaten my safety but restores my wholeness?	Withdrawing, staying quiet, turning inward	A sense of belonging and the freedom to be expressive	Safety in solitude, imagination, observation skills	Security in invisibility
The Quiet Seeker	To find meaning and connection that resonates deeply	What if I already hold the answers I've been searching for?	Seeking knowledge, staying internal, watching instead of acting	Trust in their own timing and readiness	Inner wisdom, intuitive clarity	Pride in emotional independence
The Vivacious Visionary	To create from alignment, not approval	What if my worth was never tied to what I accomplish?	Chasing success, fast-paced creation, seeking validation	Connection to their body and inner voice	Achievement, admiration, identity	Praise as a placeholder for presence
The Legacy Transformer	To know they are enough, even as they break cycles	What if breaking the cycle was always enough? Even when no one claps for it?	Carrying burdens, challenging norms, healing generational pain	Lightness, joy, and the right to simply be	Resilience, insight, emotional clarity	Identity through responsibility

BIBLIOGRAPHY

Akimoto, Kaho, et al. "Effect of 528 Hz Music on the Endocrine System and Autonomic Nervous System." Health 10, no. 9 (2018): 1159–1170. https://doi.org/10.4236/health.2018.109088

Alshami, A. M. "Pain: Is It All in the Brain or the Heart?" *Current Pain and Headache Reports* 23, no. 88 (2019). https://doi.org/10.1007/s11916-019-0827-4

Giannino, Giuseppe, et al. "The Intrinsic Cardiac Nervous System: From Pathophysiology to Therapeutic Implications." *Biology* 13, no. 2 (2024): 105. https://doi.org/10.3390/biology13020105

Maté, Gabor. *When the Body Says No: The Cost of Hidden Stress.* Toronto: Vintage Canada, 2011.

Maté, Gabor. *In the Realm of Hungry Ghosts: Close Encounters with Addiction.* Berkeley, CA: North Atlantic Books, 2010.

Segal, Inna. *The Secret Language of Your Body: The Essential Guide to Health and Wellness.* Carlsbad, CA: Hay House, 2009.

ABOUT THE AUTHOR

Anne is a licensed clinical mental health counselor (LCMHC) with a Master of Arts in Counseling and over two decades of experience walking alongside individuals as they heal trauma, unravel old patterns, and reclaim their truest selves. She is also an intuitive mentor and Reiki II practitioner, integrating clinical expertise with energy awareness, soul-deep insight, and a grounded spiritual lens.

Her debut book, *The Edge of Enough*, invites readers into the heart of transformation, where grief, grace, and the courage to love yourself like it matters (because it does) come alive on the page. Anne writes with clarity, warmth, and poetic truth-telling that mirrors the way she lives and works.

A devoted mother, nature lover, and guide for sensitive, heart-led souls, Anne brings fierce self-love, radiant presence, and an unshakable belief in possibility to all she does. With a blend of grounded wisdom and visionary spark, she meets each moment with courage, creativity, and heart. Whether supporting clients through healing and growth, teaching others to trust their inner voice, or continuing her own unfolding, she leads with compassion, authenticity, and deep reverence for the human journey.

She believes healing is holy, growth is nonlinear, and life is meant to be lived wide open with curiosity, courage, and connection.

When she is not writing or holding space for others, Anne is likely out in nature hiking or walking with her camera in hand, listening to music, lifting weights, traveling, reading, or researching something new that sparks her curiosity. She finds joy in meaningful conversations, deep laughter, and sacred moments of connection with friends, family, and those she holds dear.

YOUR VOICE MATTERS

Thank you for reading *The Edge of Enough*.
It means the world to me that you spent time with these words and walked this path alongside me.

If the book moved you, challenged you, or reminded you of something true within yourself, I would be so grateful if you shared your experience with others.

Your honest review not only helps new readers find the book, it also supports me in continuing to create meaningful and transformative work. It does not need to be long. Just a few sentences can make a real difference.

Please take a moment to leave a review on Amazon or wherever you purchased your copy.

With heartfelt thanks,
Anne

www.ingramcontent.com/pod-product-compliance
Lightning Source LLC
Chambersburg PA
CBHW021656120626
46545CB00004B/1269